SBAC
SMARTER BALANCED

GRADE 6 MATH

By Steven Krolikowski, M.A.

T0116648

About the Author

Steven Krolikowski, M.A., has been teaching mathematics in Downey, California, for more than 23 years. Seventeen of those years have been at the sixth-grade level. He holds a bachelor's of science degree, a multiple-subject teaching credential, and a master's in math education. Since 2013 he has worked closely with the Smarter Balanced Consortium and the California Department of Education. In 2013, he served as a reviewer for California's Math Adoption. In 2014, he worked with the Smarter Balanced Consortium to create the four performance levels that each student's summative assessment score falls into. In 2015, he was chosen by the California Department of Education to write and review resources for the Smarter Balanced Digital Library. In February 2016, he was featured as California's State Network Educator of the Month. In the summer of 2016, he worked closely with the director of the Smarter Balanced Consortium to create playlists of resources that match the Smarter Balanced question types. Steve Krolikowski has spoken at various major math conferences throughout the United States, and his resources can be viewed at *thinkthroughthecore.com*.

Acknowledgments

I would like to especially thank my wife, Brenda, who has inspired and supported me on a daily basis. Thanks also to my mom, and to Robert and Miguel for their continuous encouragement and advice. Finally, a special thanks to R.K., who recommended me for this opportunity.

The Smarter Balanced screenshots on page 3, as well as the Common Core Math Standards on pages 285–294, are reprinted with permission courtesy of The Regents of the University of California. The publishing of this information does not represent an endorsement of products offered or solicited by Barron's Educational Series, Inc.

© Copyright 2017 by Barron's Educational Series, Inc.

All rights reserved.
No part of this publication may be reproduced or distributed in any form or by any means without the written permission of the copyright owner.

All inquiries should be addressed to:
Barron's Educational Series, Inc.
250 Wireless Boulevard
Hauppauge, NY 11788
www.barronseduc.com

ISBN: 978-1-4380-1029-8
Library of Congress Control Number: 2017943763

Date of Manufacture: October 2017
Manufactured by: B11R11

Printed in the United States of America
9 8 7 6 5 4 3 2 1

10%
POST-CONSUMER WASTE
Paper contains a minimum of 10% post-consumer waste (PCW). Paper used in this book was derived from certified, sustainable forestlands.

Contents

Chapter 2
Ratios and Proportional Thinking   57

Chapter 3
Expressions and Equations   87

Chapter 4
Geometry   119

Chapter 5
Statistics   151

Chapter 6
Practice Test 1   187

Chapter 7
Practice Test 2   201

Introduction

What Are the Common Core Standards?

The Common Core Standards for Mathematics were created in 2009 and adopted in 2010. Before their adoption, most states used their own criteria for what should have been taught at each grade level. For various reasons, many states felt the need to create a set of standards that were common to all students across America. This way, all students across the land would be learning the same material.

The goal of the Common Core is for all students to be college and career ready as they graduate from high school. If students master the standards through high school, they should be successful in our highly competitive society.

Each grade level has its own set of mathematical standards. In sixth-grade math, these standards are clumped into categories called domains. There are five different domains, and they are illustrated as main chapters in this book. These domains include: Number Systems, Ratios and Proportional Thinking, Expressions and Equations, Geometry, and Statistics. These domains are separated into groups or clusters of individual standards. The Smarter Balanced Consortium has created a list of priority clusters (the more important standards) and supporting clusters (standards that reinforce those main standards). Although the year-end Smarter Balanced Assessment, SBAC, focuses mainly on these clusters, questions can come from many different Common Core Standards for sixth-grade math.

For details about the sixth-grade Common Core Math Standards, see Appendix A.

What Is the SBAC Test?

The Smarter Balanced Assessment Consortium is a group led by its members: 15 states, 1 territory, and the Bureau of Indian Education. The Executive Committee to this consortium oversees the development and management of the assessment system. The consortium has created the Smarter Balanced Assessment. This assessment has been created to measure the Common Core State Standards.

With these new state standards, students are working harder, thinking more critically, and applying their learning to the real world. The consortium has created a set of tests in English language arts and in mathematics for each grade level. These tests are designed to assess where students are in meeting grade-level standards. All students, including students with disabilities and English language learners, can take these tests.

The SBAC test is computer adaptive; that is, it is customized to every student. If a student answers correctly, the next question will be more difficult. Likewise, if a student gets an answer wrong, the next question will be easier. The goal of this is to challenge students so that they can perform at their highest level.

Students take the test online. In the mathematics test they must be able to write and solve problems. Although a high percentage of the problems require students to recall mathematical facts, some of the questions require higher-level critical-thinking skills. These questions measure the critical-thinking skills students will need to be college and career ready.

This test-prep book focuses on the mathematical portion of the test for sixth grade.

Computer Assessments

The year-end Smarter Balanced Assessment, SBAC, is a computer test that is taken by all students of the Smarter Balanced recognized states. It is usually given in the spring of each year. The test is given in two parts. Unlike any other test you have taken before, the entire SBAC test will be taken on the computer. You will not be able to create drawings or tables on the computer, however; these will need to be done on scratch paper.

You will have access to a variety of tools as you progress through your test. Some tools will be available at the top of your computer screen. These include a notepad, where you will be able to write down notes about the problem. You will also be able to mark each problem for review. Both tools can be very valuable if you are not sure of the solution. A basic calculator, located at the upper right of the screen, will be available for certain problems. There will also be a number pad with two different boxed sections for you to insert answers. In the CAT, or **Computer Adaptive Test**, type in your numerical responses. In the **Performance Task**, type in your constructed-response solution. You may be required to type some explanations in words.

Smarter Balanced has also set up tutorials in their practice and training tests. These can be accessed through the Smarter Balanced website: *http://www.smarterbalanced.org*

When you get to the Smarter Balanced website, click on "Assessments" at the top of the page. Drag down to "Practice and Training Tests." On the next screen, you will click on the blue icon that says "Go to the Tests!" You can then sign in as a guest. You will not need any SSID # or Session ID #.

- Just click on the sign-in icon.
- Select "Sixth-Grade" on the next screen.
- When you get to the "Your Tests" page, you have a choice of two sixth-grade practice tests or a sixth through eighth grade practice test.

As you enter any of the practice or training tests:

1. You will first come to a "Choose Settings" page. You will not need to change any of the settings for the practice test. Click on "Select" at the bottom of the screen.

2. The next page will say "Is This Your Test?" Scroll down to the bottom and click "Yes."

3. The following page will show "Instructions and Help." You can view **Test Rules for the Smarter Balanced Assessment** and another **Overview** on this page. If you still have any questions after reading through this book, information in these sections can answer them. If you are ready to begin the practice test, click on "Begin Test Now" at the bottom of the screen.

A training test has been set up for all students in grades six through eight. This test gives you a great opportunity to use the tools that are available to you. At the top of each problem are 3 straight-line segments. When you click on them, you will have access to a tutorial on how to answer the question, a mark-for-review flag, a notepad, and a strikethrough tool. At the top of the screen, you will find your calculator tool and a zoom-in or zoom-out icon. You can zoom in at any time to make the print larger. The calculator in this training test includes some buttons that are not needed for your sixth-grade test.

Types of Questions: Sample Items

The first section of the Smarter Balanced Assessment is computer adaptive. This means that if you are doing well, the questions will get more difficult. This also means that if you are not doing well, the questions will get easier. This computer adaptive section is approximately 80 percent concepts and procedures. In this section, you will be able to apply your understanding of the sixth-grade math standards in various ways. You will encounter several different types of questions: fill-in the blank, multiple response, true/false, click and drag, matching, single correct response, complete a table, and short answer. You will have plenty of opportunities to practice these types of questions throughout this book. Each computer adaptive question should take approximately 2 to 5 minutes to finish.

The second section of the test is a performance task that is also completed on a computer. You will be asked to problem solve, communicate your reasoning, and use your conceptual knowledge to develop mathematical models. Each performance task is 6 questions in length. The following definitions describe the claims that you will perform in this part of the assessment.

CLAIM 2—PROBLEM SOLVING

Students should be able to solve problems by using their previous content knowledge and problem-solving strategies.

CLAIM 3—COMMUNICATIVE REASONING

Students will come up with viable arguments to support their reasoning. They might also have to critique the reasoning of others in context.

CLAIM 4—MODELING AND DATA ANALYSIS

Students will analyze real-world situations and use mathematical models to solve problems.

 **SBAC HINT**

In the performance task, students are usually given a *stimulus, a fact statement, or a table*. Questions 1 and 2 of the performance task are usually straightforward questions that identify information from the stimulus, statement, or table. Question 3 is usually where students explain their reasoning (Claim 3). Question 4 is usually an open-ended question where students construct a mathematical model to solve a problem. Questions 5 and 6 can include any of the claims.

Each performance task measures your child's ability to solve problems while analyzing information, creating the correct mathematical model to solve a problem, communicating his or her mathematical reasoning, and using his or her knowledge of the standards to solve multistep problems.

Question Type 1: Claim 1—Concepts and Procedures

This type of question is used for approximately 80% of the computer adaptive section on the computer. This section tests your knowledge of basic mathematical operations and the sixth-grade standards.

Example 1:
Use the fact that $87 \times 392 = 34,104$.

Enter the exact product of 8.7 × 3.92: _____

Example 2:
What is the GCF for 12 and 72?

Question Type 2: Claim 3—Communicative Reasoning

These types of questions will ask you to explain or defend your reasoning. You will have to explain why you chose a particular answer choice, describe how you followed steps in a problem, or explain why a given answer is correct or not.

Example 1:

Alex and Lucy are both convinced that they have solved $4 \div \frac{1}{2}$ correctly. Alex says that the answer is 2, because he reasons that half of 4 is 2. Lucy says that the answer is 8, because she reasons that there would be 8 half-dollars in four dollars. Whose reasoning is correct? Why?

Enter your answer and your explanation in the box provided.

Example 2:

Geena says that the reflection of (3, −5) across the x-axis is (−3, −5). She reasons that if (3, −5) is reflected across the x-axis, you would change the x-value in the ordered pair to its opposite. Do you agree with Geena's reasoning? Why or why not?

Enter your answer and your explanation in the space provided below.

Question Type 3: Claims 2 and 4—Problem Solving and Modeling

These types of questions are mainly seen in the performance task portion of your assessment. They allow you to analyze a real-life scenario and create a diagram, a graph, or even an equation.

Example 1:

The local amusement park requires children to be at least 42 inches tall to ride the go-karts. Write an inequality that describes this situation.

Enter your solution in the space provided.

Example 2:

The table shows the relationship between the hours that Victor worked, *h*, and the total amount of money he earned, *d*, at his summer job.

Hours Worked	$ Earned
1	$11.25
2	$22.50
4	$45.00
8	$90.00
10	$112.50

A. Write an equation to model the relationship between the hours that Victor worked, *h*, and the amount of money, *d*, he earned.

B. Identify the dependent variable.

C. Identify the independent variable.

Calculator Use Policy

On the SBAC Assessment, you will be allowed to use a calculator to solve certain problems but not all problems. The computer adaptive section is split into two parts. The first part allows the use of an on-screen calculator, but the second part does not. You will not be able to use the calculator tool for the performance task . To use the on-screen calculator, choose the **Calculator** in the menu. The calculator will be a basic four function tool. Remember that calculators do not follow the basic order of operations. When solving an order of operations problem, make sure you follow the correct mathematical rules.

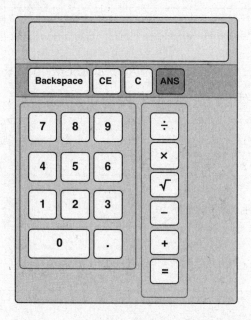

How to Use This Book: A Guide for Students

The main goal for this test-prep book is to help sixth-grade students understand the components of the Smarter Balanced Assessment. This book provides different features that will help you become familiar with the sixth-grade standards tested in the assessment. Some of the features of this book include:

- **SBAC Hints:** These hints can be found throughout the book. They are invaluable. They will help you gain more information about what you will see or need to know on the SBAC Assessment.
- **Helpful Tips:** These tips, or strategies, will help you solve procedural problems, identify key vocabulary words, increase your understanding of why problems work out the way they do, and give you some new **mnemonics**

(techniques or memorization tools) that will help you remember how to solve certain types of problems.

- **Examples:** With each standard, you are given the opportunity to see how an actual problem is worked out. One or two example problems come with each new standard.
- **Practice Problems:** Each domain standard includes practice problems that will measure your knowledge.
- **Practice Review Tests:** Each domain chapter includes a review test that is written to the **Smarter Balanced Item Specifications Document**. (This document identifies how each content standard will be addressed on the year-end assessment.) Use these practice review tests to gauge your understanding. The questions on each review test mimic the problems that were used by the Smarter Balanced Assessment Consortium to write the year-end SBAC Assessment.
- **Math Practice Tests:** Two practice tests and performance tasks have been included. These practice assessments should give you a clear picture of your strengths and weaknesses. Both practice tests mirror the types of questions you will see on the SBAC Assessment.
- **Answers and Explanations:** You can find the solutions with explanations in Chapter 8. The solutions to each standard's practice questions, chapter review tests, and the math practice tests can be found there.
- **Vocabulary:** Common Core words that are used by the writers of the SBAC Assessment are defined within the text of the book.

Parent Tips to Help Your Child Succeed

1. Encourage and motivate your child.
2. Create a plan that allows your child plenty of time to progress through this book.
3. Continue to give your child support as you monitor his/her progress.
4. If your child struggles in any section, focus his/her practice on those standards or domains with which your child is having difficulty.
5. Maintain communication with your child's teacher. The teacher might be able to give you information about your child's strengths and weaknesses.
6. Work with your child on writing short, detailed responses. Your child will be required to construct these types of responses on the SBAC Assessment.
7. Encourage your child to keep a positive attitude before the test, on test day, and after taking the test.

Grade 6 Instructional Focus

In Grade 6, instructional time should focus on four critical areas. (1) Students should connect ratios and rates to whole-number multiplication and division. They should also use ratios and rates to solve problems. (2) Students should know how to divide fractions. They should also understand that rational numbers include negative numbers. (3) Students should write, interpret, and use expressions and equations. (4) Students should develop an understanding of statistical thinking.

1. Students use reasoning about multiplication and division to solve ratio and rate problems about quantities. Students use pairs of rows (or columns) in the multiplication table to connect their understanding of multiplication and division with ratios and rates. Students analyze simple drawings that identify the size of quantities and solve a wide variety of problems involving ratios and rates. Finding the unit rate is a key sixth-grade focus as students use this to complete ratio tables, write algebraic equations, and graph ratio points on the coordinate plane.

2. Students use the meaning of fractions, the meanings of multiplication and division, and the relationship between multiplication and division to understand and explain why the procedures for dividing fractions make sense. Students use these operations to solve problems. Students extend their previous understanding of numbers and the ordering of numbers to the full system of rational numbers, which includes negative rational numbers and negative integers. They reason about the order and absolute value of rational numbers and about the location of points in all four quadrants of the coordinate plane.

3. Students understand the use of variables in mathematical expressions. They write expressions and equations that correspond to given situations, evaluate expressions, and use expressions and formulas to solve problems. Students understand that expressions in different forms can be equivalent, and they use the properties of operations to rewrite expressions in equivalent forms. Students know that the solutions of an equation are the values of the variables that make the equation true. Students use properties of operations and the idea of maintaining equality on both sides of an equation to solve simple one-step equations. Students construct and analyze tables, such as tables of quantities that are in equivalent ratios. They also use equations (such as $3x = y$) to describe relationships between quantities.

4. To build on and reinforce their understanding of numbers, students begin to develop their ability to think statistically. Students recognize that a data distribution may not have a definite center and that there are different ways to measure the center. The median measures center in the sense that it is roughly the middle value. The mean is another measure of center, but it is the average of the numbers in the data set. Students recognize that a measure of variability (interquartile range or mean absolute deviation) can also be useful when summarizing data because two very different sets of data can have the same mean and median yet be distinguished by their variability. Students learn to describe and summarize numerical data sets while considering the context in which the data were collected. They identify clusters, peaks, gaps, and symmetry. Students in Grade 6 also reason about relationships among shapes to determine area, surface area, and volume. They find areas of right triangles, other triangles, and special quadrilaterals by decomposing these shapes, rearranging or removing pieces, and relating the shapes to rectangles. By using these methods, students discuss, develop, and justify formulas for areas of triangles and parallelograms. Students find areas of polygons and surface areas of prisms and pyramids by decomposing the shapes and solids into pieces whose area they can determine. Students reason about right rectangular prisms with fractional side lengths to extend formulas for the volume of a right rectangular prism to fractional side lengths. They prepare for work on scale drawings and constructions in Grade 7 by drawing polygons in the coordinate plane.

Mathematical Practice Standards

Along with the content standards that are evident at each grade level, the Common Core has adopted practice standards that go across all grade levels. The focus of these practice standards is to give teachers a solid guide to great math instruction. We are building problem solvers through the Common Core. The focus of these practice standards is to develop mathematical thinking. The Common Core has developed these standards so that students understand why math works instead of just memorizing rules or tricks. These practice standards are the basis for a deeper understanding that will help students become college and career ready. A more detailed look at these math practice standards can be found in Appendix A.

The Common Core has eight practice standards:

1. Make sense of problems, and persevere in solving them.
2. Reason abstractly and quantitatively.
3. Construct viable arguments, and critique the reasoning of others.
4. Model with mathematics.
5. Use appropriate tools strategically.
6. Attend to precision.
7. Look for and make use of structure.
8. Look for and express regularity in repeated reasoning.

These practice standards will be more evident in the performance task section of the Smarter Balanced Assessment. Students will be asked to use tools strategically, critique mathematical reasoning, make use of patterns, or make sense of their math in typical Type 3 questions. Students must show their mathematical thinking as they progress through the year-end assessment. Using the math practice standards will allow them to do this!

Number Systems

This chapter is the first of the five domains and is the foundation of your mathematical understanding. In this chapter, you will be working on mastering basic arithmetic facts. Sixth-grade students should be able to use all four operations fluently (add, subtract, multiply, and divide) as they solve whole-number, fraction, and decimal problems. You will extend your previous knowledge of multiplication and division to divide fractions. Dividing fractions is a priority standard on the SBAC Assessment. Finally, you will apply your understanding of numbers to solve problems involving rational numbers.

Multi-Digit Division

When solving long division or multi-digit division problems, students need to have a solid understanding of how multiplication works. Division is the **inverse** (opposite operation) of multiplication. When solving a long division problem, remember that you are splitting up the **dividend** (the number that is being divided) by the **divisor** (the number that divides the dividend). Use the following steps to solve multi-digit division problems.

Steps to Divide:

- Divide
- Multiply
- Subtract
- Bring down

Example: What is the quotient of 18,936 ÷ 24?

Solution: 789

$$24\overline{)18,936}$$

18,936 is the dividend because it is the number that is being divided. The divisor is 24 because it represents the number of groups into which the dividend is being divided. The quotient is the solution in a division problem.

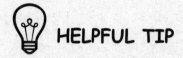 HELPFUL TIP

Using estimation might help find the first digit in the quotient.

Start by rounding 24 to 25. There are 7 quarters in $1.75. You could try 7 as the first digit in your quotient. If it is too small or too large, you can adjust it up or down.

$$
\begin{array}{r}
789 \\
24\overline{)18{,}936} \\
-16\,8 \\
\hline
2\,13 \\
-1\,92 \\
\hline
216 \\
-216 \\
\hline
0
\end{array}
$$

Remember to divide, multiply, subtract, and bring down.

1. **Divide:** 24 goes into 189 seven times. Place the 7 on top of the 9 in the dividend.
2. Then **multiply** 7 × 24, which is equivalent to 168.
3. Next **subtract** 168 from 189, which equals 21.
4. Then **bring down** the 3.
5. Find how many times 24 would go into 213.
6. This happens 8 times with 21 left over.
7. Then bring down the 6
8. Now find out how many times 24 goes into 216. This happens 9 times exactly.
9. If the divisor goes into the dividend evenly, there will not be a remainder.

The Smarter Balanced Assessment could include problems up to 5- or 6-digit dividends with 2-, 3-, 4-, or even 5-digit divisors. The assessment could also have problems either with or without remainders.

Sometimes a divisor will *not* go into a dividend evenly. A **remainder** will occur when there are no other numbers to bring down yet there is still a part of the dividend left over.

Example: Find the quotient.

$$18\overline{)329}$$

Solution: 18R5

```
       18R5
18)329
   −18↓
    149
   −144
      5
```

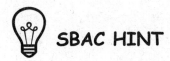

SBAC HINT

The SBAC Assessment could include word problems that require multi-digit division and problems where students must interpret the remainders.

Example: Stuart bought a gaming system for $348. He is paying for the system with 12 equal monthly payments. How much is each payment?

Solution: $29 per month. Since Stuart is dividing the total amount he paid for the system into 12 equal payments, he should divide 348 by 12. Stuart pays $29 per month for 12 months to pay off the gaming system he bought.

$$
\begin{array}{r}
29 \\
12\overline{)348} \\
-24\downarrow \\
\hline
108 \\
-108 \\
\hline
0
\end{array}
$$

Example: The sixth-grade Math Club of 174 students is planning to go on a field trip. They will be accompanied by 2 teachers and 8 chaperones. Buses can accommodate 38 people besides the bus driver. How many buses will the club need so that everyone can go on the field trip?

Solution: 5 buses. There are 184 students, parents, and teachers attending the field trip. Since each bus can accommodate 38 people, divide 184 by 38. The answer is 4R32. The Math Club will need 5 buses. The first 4 buses will each have the maximum 38 people. The remaining people (32) will need an extra bus to take them. In this problem, interpret the remainder by rounding up your answer to 5.

$$
\begin{array}{r}
4R32 \\
38\overline{)184} \\
-152 \\
\hline
32
\end{array}
$$

Practice Exercises—Multi-Digit Division

> **Common Core Standard 6.NS.B.2** Fluently divide multi-digit numbers using the standard algorithm.

Enter the exact quotient.

Divide:

1. $18\overline{)29{,}745}$ 2. $9\overline{)6{,}842}$ 3. $38\overline{)58{,}406}$ 4. $75\overline{)61{,}322}$

5. A college basketball venue sold 82,960 seats for a 16-game season. On average, how many fans attended each game?

(Answers are on page 219.)

Greatest Common Factor and Least Common Multiple

The **greatest common factor**, or **GCF**, is the largest **factor** (a number that divides evenly into another number without a remainder) that goes into two or three numbers. There are many ways to find the GCF.

One way to find the GCF is by listing all the factors in factor tables.

Example: What is the GCF of 15 and 40?

Solution: The GCF is 5.

15

1	15
3	⑤

40

1	40
2	20
4	10
⑤	8

 HELPFUL TIP

There are many ways to find the GCF, and I'm sure your teachers have shown you some of them. No matter which method you use, remember that a factor is a number that goes into another number evenly without a remainder. The GCF can never be greater than the smaller number you are comparing. In this case, the GCF cannot be greater than 15.

Another way to identify the GCF for any set of numbers is by using lists.

Example: Find the greatest common factor of 48 and 60.

48: 1, 2, 3, 4, 6, 8, ⑫ 16, 24, 48
60: 1, 2, 3, 4, 5, 6, 10, ⑫ 15, 20, 30, 60

Solution: The GCF is 12. First list the factors for both numbers. Then identify the greatest number that is common to both lists. The largest number that is common to both rows is 12.

The **least common multiple**, or **LCM**, is the smallest **multiple** (a result of multiplying a specified number by any whole number) that is common to both numbers in your set.

Example: What is the LCM of 8 and 12?

Solution: The LCM is 24. To find the LCM, start listing multiples of each number. When you get to the first multiple that is the same in both lists, you have found the LCM.

8: 8, 16, ㉔
12: 12, ㉔

Once you see that a number is common in both lists, you can stop. You have found your LCM. There is no such thing as a greatest common multiple. Multiples are **infinite** (limitless or without end).

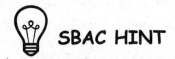 **SBAC HINT**

On the SBAC Assessment, you will be asked to find the GCF for any 2 numbers that are less than 100. You will also have to find the LCM for any two numbers that are less than or equal to 12.

Practice Exercises—Greatest Common Factor and Least Common Multiple

Common Core Standard 6.NS.B.4 Find the greatest common factor of two whole numbers less than or equal to 100 and the least common multiple of two whole numbers less than or equal to 12. Use the distributive property to express a sum of two whole numbers 1–100 with a common factor as a multiple of a sum of two whole numbers with no common factor. *For example, express 36 + 8 as 4(9 + 2).*

1. Find the GCF of 25 and 90.

2. Find the LCM of 4 and 10.

3. Find the GCF of 17 and 68.

4. Becky braids her hair every 6 days and paints her nails every 9 days. Today is June 1, and she braided her hair and painted her nails. On what date will she braid her hair and paint her nails again?

5. Consider the equation showing the distributive property.

Enter the unknown value that would make the equation true.

$$48 + 60 = 12(\_\_ + 5)$$

(Answers are on page 219.)

Division of Fractions

When dividing fractions, it is important to remember that you are finding how many times the **divisor** (the number by which the dividend is being divided) goes into the **dividend** (the number that is divided).

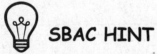 **SBAC HINT**

On the Smarter Balanced Assessment, you will divide fractions by fractions, divide whole numbers or mixed numbers by fractions, and identify a missing dividend or divisor in an equation.

You must understand the following three concepts from prior grades to truly grasp division of fractions.

1. **Grouping.** Sometimes, looking for groups can simplify division. For instance, if you divide 12 ÷ 6 = 2, you can also look at this problem as 6 groups of 2. The quotient, or answer in the division problem, identifies how many are going to be in each group.

The same rationale applies to dividing fractions, such as $\frac{1}{2} \div \frac{1}{4} = 2$.

This means that you have 2 groups of $\frac{1}{4}$, which is equivalent to $\frac{1}{2}$.

$\frac{1}{2}$	$\frac{1}{2}$

$\frac{1}{4}$	$\frac{1}{4}$	$\frac{1}{4}$	$\frac{1}{4}$

Another way of looking at $\frac{1}{2} \div \frac{1}{4} = 2$ is with money. Two groups of $0.25, or $\frac{1}{4}$ of a dollar, is equivalent to $0.50, or $\frac{1}{2}$ of a dollar.

2. **Multiplication of Fractions.** Since multiplication is the opposite of division, we can work backward to understand better how to divide fractions. From the previous example, you can see that two groups of one-fourth equal one-half: $2 \times \frac{1}{4} = \frac{1}{2}$. In fact, you can see that using multiplication will help you solve any division problem involving fractions or mixed numbers. Remember the following from fifth grade. When you multiply fractions, multiply the numerators by the numerators and the denominators by the denominators to get the answer.

Example: Multiply $\frac{3}{8} \times \frac{1}{2}$.

$$\frac{3}{8} \times \frac{1}{2} = \frac{3}{16}$$

Solution: $\frac{3}{16}$. When multiplying fractions, multiply across the top and across the bottom to get the solution.

HELPFUL TIP

Multiplication is the opposite of division. So if you multiply by the **reciprocal** (the inverted or flipped over fraction from its original form), you will get the correct solution in any problem that divides a number by a fraction. The reciprocal of any number x is $\frac{1}{x}$.

Here are some examples of reciprocals:

- The reciprocal of $\frac{3}{7}$ is $\frac{7}{3}$.

- The reciprocal of 9 is $\frac{1}{9}$ because 9 can be written as $\frac{9}{1}$.

Be careful when changing a mixed number to its reciprocal. First change the mixed number into an improper fraction.

Example: Change $2\frac{5}{8}$ into an improper fraction.

Solution: $\frac{21}{8}$. Use the following steps when changing a mixed number into an improper fraction:

STEP 1   Keep the same denominator. In this case, the denominator of 8 will stay the same.

STEP 2   To find the new numerator, multiply the whole number by the denominator and add the original numerator to that product. In this case, 2 times 8 equals 16 and 16 plus 5 equals 21.

$$2\frac{5}{8} = \frac{21}{8}$$

- The reciprocal of $4\frac{1}{5}$ is $\frac{5}{21}$. This is correct because $4\frac{1}{5}$ is equivalent to $\frac{21}{5}$ and the reciprocal of $\frac{21}{5}$ is $\frac{5}{21}$.

 **HELPFUL TIP**

To divide a fraction, **keep** the first fraction the same, **change** the division sign into a multiplication sign, and **flip** over the second fraction (its reciprocal). The reciprocal is also called the "multiplicative inverse." A way to remember this tip is to Keep, Change, and Flip.

Example: $\frac{3}{8} \div \frac{1}{2}$

Solution: $\frac{3}{4}$

$$\frac{3}{8} \div \frac{1}{2}$$

$$\frac{3}{8} \times \frac{2}{1}$$

$$\frac{3}{8} \times \frac{2}{1} = \frac{6}{8}$$

$$\frac{6}{8} \div \frac{2}{2} = \frac{3}{4}$$

Keep the first fraction $\frac{3}{8}$. Change the division sign into a multiplication sign. Flip over the second fraction to form its reciprocal: $\frac{1}{2}$ becomes $\frac{2}{1}$. Then multiply across and simplify.

You might be asked to divide mixed or whole numbers by fractions. To do this, first change any mixed or whole numbers into improper fractions. Then use the same steps listed above to divide the second fraction into the first fraction.

- To change whole numbers into improper fractions, write the whole number over 1. For example, $12 = \frac{12}{1}$.

- To change a mixed number into an improper fraction, keep the denominator the same. To get the numerator, multiply the whole number by the denominator and add the original numerator. An example of this is $5\frac{3}{4} = \frac{23}{4}$. The denominator of 4 stayed the same. To find the numerator, multiply 5×4 and then add 3 to that total.

Example: $2\frac{1}{4} \div \frac{3}{8}$

Solution: 6. $\frac{9}{4} \div \frac{3}{8} = \frac{9}{4} \times \frac{8}{3} = \frac{72}{12} = 6$. First change the mixed number into an improper fraction $2\frac{1}{4} = \frac{9}{4}$. **Keep** the first fraction, $\frac{9}{4}$. **Change** the division sign into a multiplication sign. **Flip** the second fraction, $\frac{3}{8}$, to its reciprocal, $\frac{8}{3}$. Then either reduce first and multiply across, or multiply across and then reduce.

3. **Identifying a Missing Dividend or Divisor.** On the Smarter Balanced Assessment, students will solve for missing dividends or divisors. You must identify if the solution calls for multiplying or dividing the two given fractions.

Example: Find the missing dividend: ___ $\div \frac{2}{3} = \frac{1}{5}$

Solution: $\frac{2}{15}$. When the dividend is missing, multiply the two other fractions by each other.

$$\frac{2}{3} \times \frac{1}{5} = \frac{2}{15}$$

You might be asking, "How do you know whether to multiply or divide the two fractions?" Let's use some whole numbers to find out.

$$10 \div 2 = 5$$

We also know that $5 \times 2 = 10$. In any division problem, work backward and use multiplication to find the missing dividend or divisor.

Example: Find the missing divisor: $\frac{3}{8} \div$ _____ $= \frac{3}{4}$

Solution: $\frac{1}{2}$. From the previous problem, you found out that $10 \div 2 = 5$. You also know from previous grades that $10 \div 5 = 2$. Divide the last fraction from the first fraction to get the missing divisor. Remember to Keep, Change, and Flip.

$$\frac{3}{8} \div \frac{3}{4}$$

$$\frac{3}{8} \times \frac{4}{3}$$

$$\frac{12}{24} \text{ or } \frac{1}{2}$$

Practice Exercises—Division of Fractions

Common Core Standard 6.NS.A.1 Interpret and compute quotients of fractions, and solve word problems involving division of fractions by fractions, e.g., by using visual fraction models and equations to represent the problem. *For example, create a story context for* $\left(\frac{2}{3}\right) \div \left(\frac{3}{4}\right)$ *and use a visual fraction model to show the quotient; use the relationship between multiplication and division to explain that* $\left(\frac{2}{3}\right) \div \left(\frac{3}{4}\right) = \frac{8}{9}$ *because* $\left(\frac{3}{4}\right)$ *of* $\left(\frac{8}{9}\right)$ *is* $\left(\frac{2}{3}\right)$. *(In general,* $\left(\frac{a}{b}\right) \div \left(\frac{c}{d}\right) = \frac{ad}{bc}$.*)* *How much chocolate will each person get if 3 people share* $\frac{1}{2}$ *lb. of chocolate equally? How many* $\frac{3}{4}$*-cup servings are in* $\frac{2}{3}$ *of a cup of yogurt? How wide is a rectangular strip of land with length* $\frac{3}{4}$ *mi and area* $\frac{1}{2}$ *square mi?*

1. What is the reciprocal of $\frac{5}{9}$?

2. What is the reciprocal of $4\frac{2}{3}$?

3. $\frac{4}{5} \div \frac{1}{5} =$ _____

4. $8\frac{1}{2} \div \frac{1}{4} =$ _____

5. Divide: $\frac{2}{3} \div$ _____ $= \frac{16}{21}$

6. Divide: _____ $\div \frac{1}{4} = \frac{5}{6}$

7. Circle the letter that best illustrates how to use the inverse operation of $\frac{5}{7} \div \frac{3}{8}$ correctly.

   A. $\frac{7}{5} \times \frac{8}{3}$

   B. $\frac{5}{7} \times \frac{8}{3}$

   C. $\frac{5}{7} \times \frac{3}{8}$

(Answers are on pages 219–220.)

Decimal Operations

Adding and subtracting decimals are covered in earlier grades. You should be able to solve these types of problems fluently in sixth grade. To understand adding and subtracting decimals, you must have a firm grasp of the place value system.

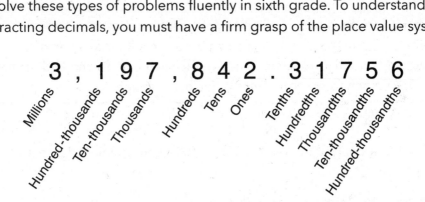

Teachers have probably pointed out in earlier grades that you need to line up the decimal points when adding or subtracting decimals. They did this to stress the importance of adding and subtracting the same place values. You can add or subtract numbers only if they have the same place value.

Example: Bob earned $108.00 on Friday and $73.00 on Saturday. How much money did Bob earn altogether?

Solution: $181.00. After lining up the decimal points and place values correctly, add down from right to left. Make sure to carry the 1 when adding 8 and 3 together.

The correct and incorrect ways of how to solve an addition of decimal problem are shown below. If you don't line up the decimal points and add the numbers straight down, you will get $838.00–which is wrong.

A. Incorrect Way:	108.00		**B. Correct Way:**	1 108.00
	+ 73.000			+ 73.00
	838.00			181.00

Problem A is incorrect because adding 108 to 73 cannot result in a solution of 838. You can see that adding 1 hundred to 7 tens is not equivalent to 8 hundreds. Problem B is correct because all the same place values are being added together.

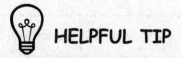 **HELPFUL TIP**

Adding or subtracting decimals might require you to add one or more zeros at the end of some numbers. This keeps everything lined up. You will also need to add a decimal point to the end of any whole number to change it into a decimal number.

Example: Isabella bought a notebook for $2.97, a box of colored pencils for $3.40, and a ruler for $0.87.

Part A: What is the total amount of the items?

Solution: $7.24

$$
\begin{array}{r}
2\ 1\ \ \\
2.97 \\
3.40 \\
+\ 0.87 \\
\hline
\$7.24
\end{array}
$$

Part B: If Isabella paid with a $20 gift card, how much money should she receive in change?

Solution: $12.76

$$
\begin{array}{r}
1\ 9\ 9_1 \\
20.00 \\
-\ \ 7.24 \\
\hline
\$12.76
\end{array}
$$

Multiplication of decimals does not require lining up the decimal points. Let's look at two methods to solve these types of problems.

1. **Estimation by Rounding**

   Multiply: 3.2×19.8

   Start by rounding both numbers to the nearest whole number. Then multiply 3×20, which is equal to 60.

Now take the decimal points out of the original problem, and then multiply 198 × 32.

$$
\begin{array}{r}
2\,2 \\
1\,1 \\
198 \\
\times\ 32 \\
\hline
396 \\
+\ 5940 \\
\hline
6336
\end{array}
$$

Let's go back and look at your estimate of 60. The solution to the problem is 6336, without decimal points. Place your decimal in the **product** (the answer in a multiplication problem) between each of the 3s. The decimal is placed here because 63.36 is the nearest value to your estimate of 60.

2. **Counting the Digits After the Decimal Points in the Factors.** Another way to make sure that you have placed the decimal point in the right spot is to count how many decimal places each **factor** (numbers that can be multiplied together to get another number) has.

   In the problem 3.2 × 19.8, the first factor has one digit after the decimal point, and the second factor also has one digit after the decimal point.

   After multiplying, place the decimal in your product. Since there are a total of two numbers after the decimal points based on both factors, start at the end of the product and move the decimal in two places to the left.

HELPFUL TIP

To decrease the decimal places in a number, multiply by a power of 10. For example: 3.28 × 100 = 328. When you increase the decimal places in a number, you are just dividing by that same power of 10. For example: 328 ÷ 100 = 3.28.

When **dividing decimals**, you cannot be left with a remainder. You will continue to divide and bring down zeros until the solution either **terminates** or **repeats**.

💡 SBAC HINT

When dividing decimals on the SBAC Assessment, solutions will not go further than the thousandths place.

- When a decimal point is only in the dividend, move the decimal point straight up and divide.

  Example: Divide: 1.008 ÷ 12

  Solution: 0.084

$$
\begin{array}{r}
0.084 \\
12\overline{)1.008} \\
-96\downarrow \\
\hline
48 \\
-48 \\
\hline
0
\end{array}
$$

- When there is a decimal point in the divisor, first move that decimal point to the end of the divisor. Remember to count how many places to the right that you move the decimal point. Then do the same with the dividend. Move its decimal point the same number of places to the right. Finally, bring the decimal point straight up and divide.

  Example: Divide: $4.5\overline{)39.6}$

  Solution: 8.8. Move the decimal point in 4.5 to the right side of the number. This is done because it is easier to divide by an integer than by a decimal number. Since you moved the decimal point one place in the divisor, you will move it one place to the right in the dividend. So 4.5 will become 45 and 39.6 will become 396.0. Now you are ready to divide.

$$
\begin{array}{r}
8.8 \\
45\overline{)396.0} \\
-360\downarrow \\
\hline
36\ 0 \\
-36\ 0 \\
\hline
0
\end{array}
$$

Practice Exercises—Decimal Operations

> **Common Core Standard 6.NS.B.3** Fluently add, subtract, multiply, and divide multi-digit decimals using the standard algorithm for each operation.

Enter the exact sum or difference.

1. 289.67 – 43.9

2. 18.8 + 12 + 3.905

3. Bob spent $47.42 on a pair of headphones. He gave the cashier $50.00. How much change did Bob receive?

4. Tammy wanted to purchase sweaters for her three puppies. A table of costs per sweater has been created.

Type of Dog	Cost of Sweater
Pekingese	$12.99
Dachshund	$12.95
Chihuahua	$13.50

Use the table to answer the following:

Tammy has a total of $40.00 to spend on the three sweaters. Does she have enough money to purchase all three sweaters? Why or why not?

5. Check all the following expressions that are equivalent to 0.65.

___ 0.25 – 0.90

___ 0.47 + 0.28

___ 0.3 + 0.35

___ 0.39 + 0.26

___ 0.8 – 0.15

6. 45.2 × 0.36

7. 292.4 ÷ 17

8. Use the fact that 37 × 421 = 15,577. Enter the exact product of 3.7 × 42.1.

9. The area of a rectangular vegetable garden is 34.2 square feet. The width is 4.8 feet. What is the length of the vegetable garden?

10. $0.04 \overline{)1.26}$

(Answers are on pages 220–221.)

Rational Numbers on a Number Line and Absolute Value

In sixth grade, students extend their knowledge of numbers to include **rational numbers** (any number that can be written as a fraction). These are numbers that include positive and negative whole numbers as well as fractions where the denominator is not zero.

Students will be required to use rational numbers to represent quantities in context, place or position rational numbers on a number line, compare rational numbers by using inequalities, and identify a rational number's **absolute value** (a number's distance from zero). Students will be asked to identify certain positive or negative whole numbers in the context of temperatures, elevation changes, credits or debits, and positive/negative electrical charges.

Example: The temperature at noon in Michigan was 12 degrees below zero. Identify the integer that represents the temperature in degrees, and explain the meaning of zero in this situation.

Solution: –12. The meaning of zero is the temperature scale in degrees. To identify the meaning of zero, think of the unit that is being described in the problem.

Example: A shark swam at a depth of thirty feet below the surface of the water. Identify the meaning of zero as it pertains to the shark.

Solution: The meaning of zero in this problem is sea level. Since the example is showing a specific elevation that the shark is swimming at, sea level identifies all elevations in relation to zero.

A great way to rank or position positive or negative whole numbers is to create a number line. Placing zero in the middle of your number line can help you better understand where the numbers will go. Positive numbers will always be placed to the right of zero, and negative numbers will always be placed to the left of zero.

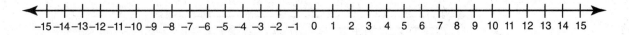

Students will be asked to use the number line to do the following:

- Identify where numbers are placed on the number line in order to answer true/false statements.
- Identify where rational numbers are placed on the number line.
- Place numbers from least to greatest on the number line.

Example: Use the number line to complete the table below. Select True or False for each statement.

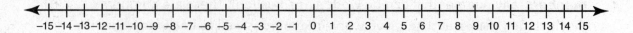

Statement	True	False
The number 12 is to the right of −4.		
The numbers −7 and 9 are both located to the left of zero.		
The number −13 is located to the right of −5.		

Solution:

Statement	True	False	Reason
The number 12 is to the right of −4.	X		All positive numbers are to the right of all negative numbers.
The numbers −7 and 9 are both located to the left of zero.		X	Only negative numbers are to the left of zero.
The number −13 is located to the right of −5.		X	When comparing two negative integers, the number closer to zero is to the right of the other negative integer.

Example: Place the following numbers into the correct boxes on the number line.

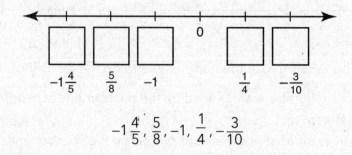

$$-1\frac{4}{5}, \frac{5}{8}, -1, \frac{1}{4}, -\frac{3}{10}$$

Solution:

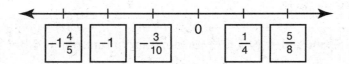

$-1\frac{4}{5}$ goes into the first box on the left. Then from left to right, −1 goes into the second box. $-\frac{3}{10}$ goes into the third box. $\frac{1}{4}$ goes into the next box. Finally, $\frac{5}{8}$ goes into the box all the way to the right.

Absolute value is measured as a number's distance from zero. To find the absolute value of any number, count the number of spaces that number is from zero. The symbol for absolute value is | |. Whether you are looking at positive or negative integers does not matter; the absolute value of any number is its distance from zero. A bird flying at 70 feet above zero could be represented by $|70|$. The distance the bird is from the ground is 70 feet. A shark swimming at 40 feet below sea level can be shown as $|{-40}|$. The actual distance the shark is from zero is 40 feet. Since you cannot travel a distance that is negative, the solution to any number's distance from zero, which is its absolute value, is always positive.

Opposites have the same absolute value, and they are both the same distance from zero. The numbers −5 and +5 are opposites since they are both 5 numbers away from zero. The $|{-5}| = 5$, and the $|5| = 5$. The absolute values of opposite numbers are always equivalent.

Example: Evaluate: $|{-13}|$

Solution: 13. The absolute value of any number is its distance from zero. Since −13 is 13 numbers away from zero, its absolute value is 13.

Example: What is the opposite of the opposite of negative 5?

Solution: −5. The opposite of the opposite of any number is the number itself. The opposite of a negative is a positive. If you then take the opposite of that, it is right back to being a negative.

Practice Exercises—Rational Numbers on a Number Line and Absolute Value

Common Core Standard 6.NS.C.6 Understand a rational number as a point on the number line. Extend number line diagrams and coordinate axes familiar from previous grades to represent points on the line and in the plane with negative number coordinates.

Common Core Standard 6.NS.C.6.A Recognize opposite signs of numbers as indicating locations on opposite sides of 0 on the number line; recognize that the opposite of the opposite of a number is the number itself, e.g., –(–3) = 3, and that 0 is its own opposite.

Common Core Standard 6.NS.C.7 Understand ordering and absolute value of rational numbers.

Common Core Standard 6.NS.C.7.C Understand the absolute value of a rational number as its distance from 0 on the number line; interpret absolute value as magnitude for a positive or negative quantity in a real-world situation. *For example, for an account balance of -30 dollars, write |–30| = 30 to describe the size of the debt in dollars.*

1. List the following numbers in order from least to greatest.

$$-7, |-5|, -2, 0, |-3|, -4$$

2. Use the number line to place the following rational numbers into the correct boxes.

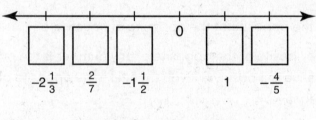

$$-2\frac{1}{3}, \frac{2}{7}, -1\frac{1}{2}, 1, -\frac{4}{5}$$

3. Use the number line to complete the table below. Select True or False for each statement.

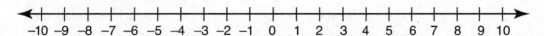

Statement	True	False
5 is located to the right of |−8|.		
The opposite of the opposite of −4 = 4.		
−|9| = −9.		

4. What is the opposite of −12?

5. List the following numbers from greatest to least.

$$-3, 2, -1.5, -2, 0$$

(Answers are on pages 221–222.)

Graphing Points on a Coordinate Plane

Students will need to understand the **coordinate plane**, which is a four-quadrant grid created by intersecting vertical and horizontal number lines. The horizontal number line is called the **x-axis**, and the vertical number line is called the **y-axis**. The four **quadrants** (infinite regions created by the intersection of the x-axis and y-axis) are made up of an infinite number of **ordered pairs**. Ordered pairs are two numbers written in a specific order to specify a point on the coordinate plane. The first number represents the x-value of the point, and the second number represents the y-value. There are four quadrants. Quadrant I is where both the x- and y-values are positive (+, +). Quadrant II is to the left of Quadrant I. Quadrant II contains ordered pairs where the x-value is negative and the y-value is positive (−, +). In Quadrant III, both the x- and y-values are negative (−, −). The final section is Quadrant IV, where the x-value is positive but the y-value is negative (+, −).See the coordinate plane below.

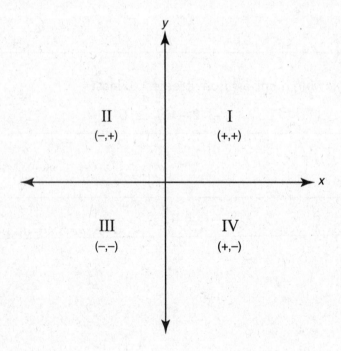

 SBAC HINT

You will be required to name quadrants, identify and plot ordered pairs, find the distance between two ordered pairs with the same x- or y-values, and find reflections of specific ordered pairs across the x- or y-axis lines.

When naming quadrants, you must look at the signs in the ordered pair.

Example: Identify the quadrant for (–3, 6).

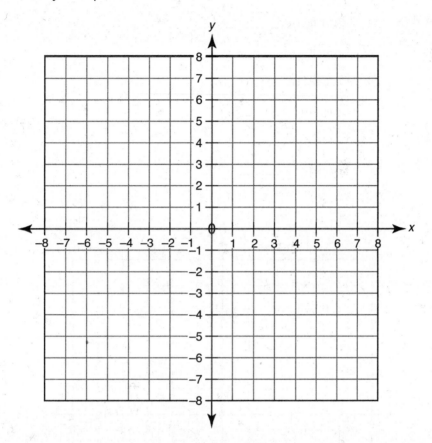

Solution: (–3, 6) lies in Quadrant II. Any ordered pair that includes a negative x-value and a positive y-value lies in Quadrant II.

When plotting or identifying points on the coordinate plane, you start at the **origin**, which is the point where the horizontal and vertical axes cross. The first number in an ordered pair indicates the left or right movement along the x-axis (horizontal axis). The second number in an ordered pair indicates the up or down movement along the y-axis (vertical axis).

Example: Plot the following points on the coordinate plane below. Label the points by the corresponding letter. Identify the quadrant where each point is found.

Point A (5, −1)   Quadrant: _____

Point B (−3, −2)   Quadrant: _____

Point C (−4, 5)   Quadrant: _____

Point D (4, 2)   Quadrant: _____

Point E (−1, −3)   Quadrant: _____

Point F (2, −5)   Quadrant: _____

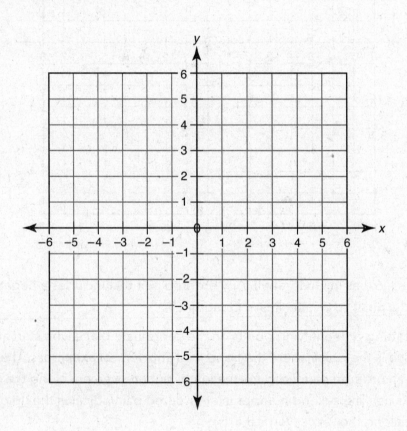

Solutions:

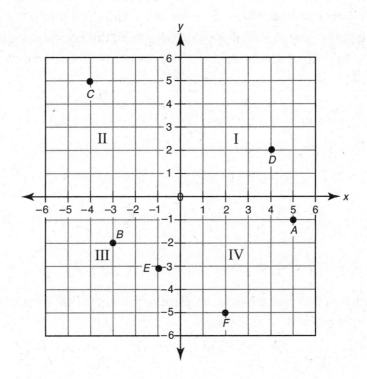

Point A (5, −1) lies in Quadrant IV. Point B (−3, −2) lies in Quadrant III. Point C (−4, 5) lies in Quadrant II. Point D (4, 2) lies in Quadrant I. Point E (−1, −3) lies in Quadrant III. Point F (2, −5) lies in Quadrant IV.

 **HELPFUL TIP**

When the first number in an ordered pair is 0, the point lies on the y-axis. When the second number is 0, the point lies on the x-axis.

- The ordered pair (0, −4) is not in a quadrant. It lies on the y-axis because the first number is 0.
- The ordered pair (5, 0) is not in a quadrant. It lies on the x-axis because the second number is 0.

Practice Exercises—Graphing Points on a Coordinate Plane

Common Core Standards 6.NS.C.8 Solve real-world and mathematical problems by graphing points in all four quadrants of the coordinate plane. Include use of coordinates and absolute value to find distances between points with the same first coordinate or the same second coordinate.

1. Put a check next to all the ordered pairs that lie in Quadrant II.

   Point A (–6, –3) _____

   Point B (5, –7) _____

   Point C (–3, 1) _____

   Point D (7, 4) _____

   Point E (–5, 2) _____

2. Use the coordinate plane below to identify the letter that matches the corresponding point.

   Point A (6, –5)   Point B (–6, –5)   Point C (–6, 5)

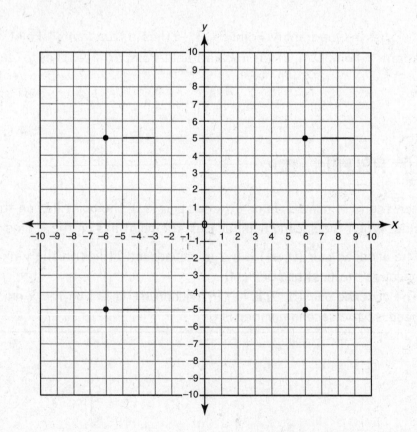

3. Plot each ordered pair on the coordinate plane.

Point A $\left(1\frac{1}{2}, -2\right)$

Point B $(0, -1.5)$

Point C $\left(-1\frac{1}{2}, -1\frac{1}{2}\right)$

Point D $(-2, 0)$

Point E $\left(-\frac{1}{2}, 1\right)$

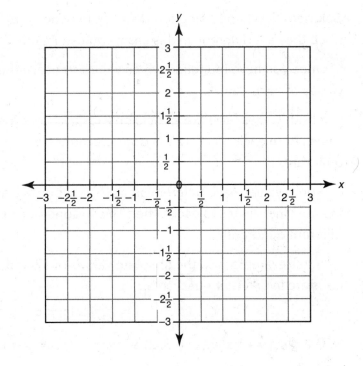

(Answers are on pages 222–223.)

Distance

In addition to identifying points and quadrants on the SBAC Assessment, you will have to identify the distance between two points on the coordinate plane. You can find the distance between points using two different methods.

 **SBAC HINT**

The distance between two points can be found by using the absolute value or by just counting from one point to another.

The first method uses absolute value. When two points have the same x-value (x-coordinate), they create or form a vertical line. When two points have the same y-value (y-coordinate), they create a horizontal line. When using absolute value to find the distance between points, make sure to use the values (x or y), that are different.

Example: Find the distance between (–6, 2) and (–6, –7).

Solution: 9. When finding the distance between (–6, 2) and (–6, –7), use the *y*-values since they are different. In this case, you use 2 and –7.

Once you have identified which values to use, either add or subtract the absolute values of each number.

If both values have the same sign (positive or negative), subtract the absolute values from each other. This is done because both ordered pairs are in the same quadrant.

If both values have different signs (one is positive and one is negative), add the absolute values to each other. This is done because both ordered pairs lie in different quadrants.

In this example, add the absolute values of –7 and 2 because the two ordered pairs are in different quadrants.

$$|-7| + |2| = 9$$

The distance between (–6, 2) and (–6, –7) is 9. Remember that distance is always positive!

Example: What is the distance between the points (3, –2) and (3, –8)?

Solution: 6. Since the signs of –8 and –2 are the same, subtract their absolute values.

$$|-8| - |-2| = 6$$

Example: Find the distance between (–6, 4) and (3, 4).

Solution: 9. Since the signs on –6 and 3 are different, add their absolute values.

$$|-6| + |3| = 9$$

The second way to find the distance between any two points is to count from one point to another. This is by far the easier way. However, sometimes a coordinate plane might not be accessible.

 **HELPFUL TIP**

Make sure that when you count the distance between two points, do not count the starting point as one. It is zero.

Practice Exercises—Distance

Common Core Standards 6.NS.C.8 Solve real-world and mathematical problems by graphing points in all four quadrants of the coordinate plane. Include use of coordinates and absolute value to find distances between points with the same first coordinate or the same second coordinate.

1. Use the following coordinate plane.

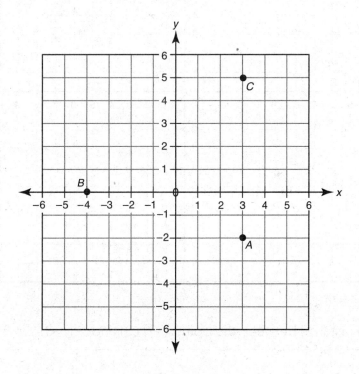

Find the distance between points *A* and *C*.

2. Use the following coordinate plane.

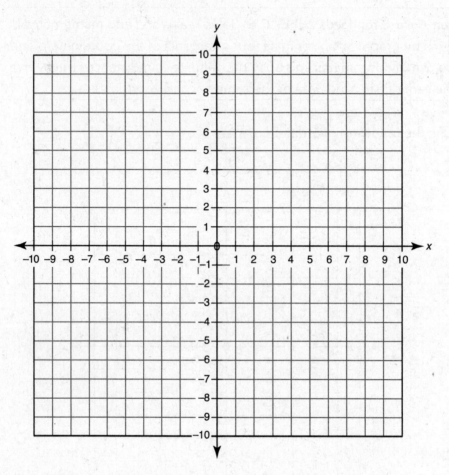

Find the distance between the points (−7, −3) and (−1, −3).

3. Consider the following two ordered pairs, point A (–3, 2) and point B (5, 2).

   Part A: Write an absolute value expression that identifies the distance between points A and B.

4. Matthew thinks that the distance between the points (–4, 6) and (–4, 1) is 7 units. He added the absolute values of 6 and 1 to get an answer of 7. Bailey believes that the distance between the two points is 5. She subtracted the absolute values of 6 and 1 to get an answer of 5. Which student is correct and why?

   Part B: Solve the expression.

(Answers are on page 223.)

Reflections

A **reflection** is a transformation where a point is moved to an equal distance on the opposite side of a given line. Reflections will be covered on the SBAC Assessment. When finding reflection points, you must first identify if the existing ordered pair is being reflected across (over) the x-axis or the y-axis. There are a couple of ways to find the reflection point across the x-axis or the y-axis.

- A coordinate plane can be used to find the reflection point. For example, you want to find the reflection of (−3, 5) across the y-axis. First you plot the initial point. This point lies in Quadrant II. By crossing the y-axis, the new point lies in Quadrant I. You might want to draw a line across the y-axis so that you can visually see that the point is being reflected correctly. The new point (the reflection point) is (3, 5).

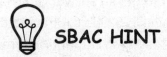 **SBAC HINT**

You can check your new reflection point by folding your paper along the axis line over which the point is reflected. If you fold your paper and the two points are on top of each other, your new reflection point is correct. Both the original point and its reflection point will be **equidistant** (the same distance) to the axis line.

- The second way to find a reflection point from its original plotted point is to change one of the values in your ordered pair. For example, if you want to find the reflection of (5, 2) over the x-axis, change the y-value to its opposite. In this case, the new reflection point is (5, −2). You could again check your solution by plotting the two points and seeing if they are equidistant from the x-axis. If you wanted to reflect (5, 2) over the y-axis, then just change the x-value to its opposite: (−5, 2).

Example: Find the reflection of (7, 1) across the y-axis.

Solution: (−7, 1). The reflection can be found by taking the opposite of the x-value in the ordered pair. The x-value is 7, and its opposite is −7. The two points, (7, 1) and (−7, 1), are equidistant from the y-axis.

Practice Exercises—Reflections

> **Common Core Standard 6.NS.C.6.B** Understand signs of numbers in ordered pairs as indicating locations in quadrants of the coordinate plane; recognize that when two ordered pairs differ only by signs, the locations of the points are related by reflections across one or both axes.

1. The points (7, −5) and (−3, 1) are going to be reflected across the *x*-axis. Complete the table to show the coordinates of the new reflection points across the *x*-axis. You may use the coordinate plane below to help find the new reflection points.

Original Point	Coordinates of Point After Reflection Over *x*-axis
(7, -5)	
(-3, 1)	

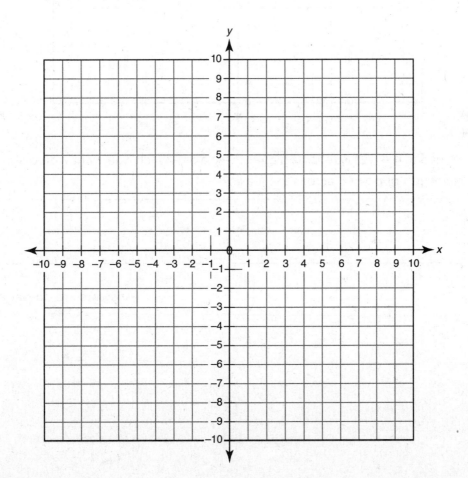

2. Use the following coordinate plane.

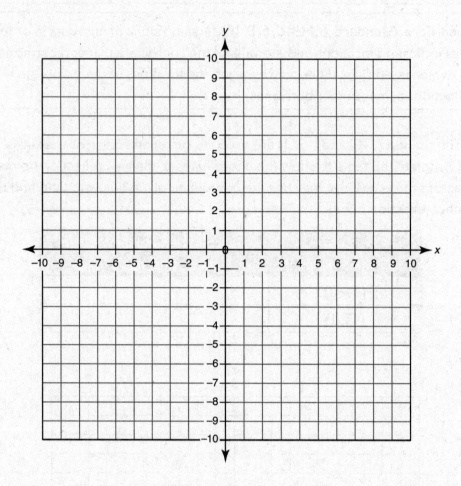

Point S at (–4, –2) is reflected over the y-axis. Which quadrant would show the reflection of point S across the y-axis?

(Answers are on page 224.)

PRACTICE REVIEW TEST:
Number Systems

1. Enter the exact difference: 567.82 – 29.14

2. Fill in the blank: 60 + 72 = 12(_____ + 6)

3. Use the fact that 29 × 568 = 16,472.

   Enter the exact product of 2.9 × 5.68.

4. 29,344 ÷ 66

5. What is the opposite of the opposite of –9?

6. What is the greatest common factor of 50 and 75?

7. Fill in the missing value: $\frac{1}{3} \div$ _____ $= \frac{4}{9}$

8. Check all the expressions that are equivalent to 0.71.

_____ 0.3 + 0.31

_____ 0.9 − 0.19

_____ 0.65 + 0.6

_____ 1 − 0.31

_____ 0.6 + 0.11

9. Complete the table. Select True or False for each statement.

Statement	True	False
The number −8 is located to the right of 10 on the number line.		
The number −7 is located to the right of −15 on the number line.		
|−7.9| is located to the left of 7.45 on the number line.		

10. What is the least common multiple of 6 and 9?

11. Identify all the following points from Quadrant II. Check all that apply.

    A. _____ (−3, 8)

    B. _____ (5, −7)

    C. _____ (−4, 1)

    D. _____ (−2, −9)

12. Complete the table to identify if the values make the inequality $x < 9$ true or false.

Number	True	False
$|-10|$		
7		
$-5\frac{7}{8}$		
$-(-12)$		

13. Which expression is equivalent to $\frac{7}{9} \div \frac{5}{6}$? Check the appropriate expression.

    A. _____ $\frac{7}{9} \times \frac{5}{6}$

    B. _____ $\frac{9}{7} \times \frac{6}{5}$

    C. _____ $\frac{7}{9} \times \frac{6}{5}$

14. Enter the exact quotient: 0.014 ÷ 0.05

15. −4.2 is to the right of −10 on the number line. Write an inequality that compares the two quantities.

16. Rewrite the following numbers from smallest to greatest:

$$-3.4, 0, -2.8, -5, -\frac{3}{4}$$

17. Matthew says that the distance between (7, −2) and (−4, −2) is 3. He reasons that 7 − 4 = 3. Do you agree with Matthew? Explain your reasoning.

18. Two points, (−4, 5) and (−3, −2), will be reflected across the y-axis. Fill in the missing reflection points in the table below. You may use the coordinate plane below to help you find the reflection points.

Coordinate Points	New Coordinate Point After Reflection Across the y-axis
(−4, 5)	
(−3, −2)	

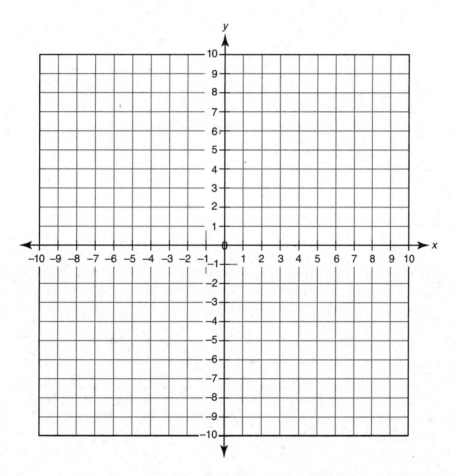

(Answers are on pages 224–226.)

Ratios and Proportional Thinking

This chapter is the second of the five domains, and it serves as the foundation for proportional thinking throughout middle school and high school. In this chapter, you will look at the relationships between numbers. Other standards that you will focus on include understanding the concept of a ratio and unit rate, completing tables of equivalent ratios, finding a percent of a quantity, and using ratio reasoning to convert measurement units.

Ratios

Ratios are a way to compare two different quantities using division. They also identify the relationship between those quantities.

Example: There are 12 boys and 13 girls in your math class. What is the ratio of boys to girls?

Solution: The ratio of boys to girls is 12 to 13. You could also say that the relationship between boys and girls is that for every 12 boys, you have 13 girls.

Ratios can be written 3 different ways. In the above example, the ratio of boys to girls could be written as:

$$12 \text{ to } 13 \qquad 12:13 \qquad \text{or} \qquad \frac{12 \text{ boys}}{13 \text{ girls}}$$

 **HELPFUL TIP**

Since the two numbers in a ratio identify a specific relationship, it is important to put them in the correct order. The above example refers to the ratio of boys to girls. Writing that ratio as 13:12 would be incorrect.

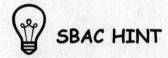 **SBAC HINT**

The SBAC Assessment does not require you to label your units when identifying a ratio.

In the previous example of boys to girls, the relationship is a **part to part ratio**. That type of ratio compares one unit to another unit where both units are part of the total. In the previous example, both units (boys and girls) are parts of the whole class. If a question asked for the ratio of boys to total students instead, it would be a **part to whole ratio**. That type of ratio compares one unit (boys) to the total number of units combined (the whole class).

Remember that when you are asked to identify the total amount, or whole, you need to add together *all* the quantities. This includes the first quantity in the ratio.

Example: Jolie invited 14 girls and 9 boys to her birthday party. Is the ratio of boys to the total number of girls and boys considered a part to part ratio or a part to whole ratio?

Solution: It is a part to whole ratio. The ratio is part to whole because the comparison is between part of the total (boys) and the total number of friends (boys and girls) Jolie invited.

Practice Exercises—Ratios

Common Core Standard 6.RP.A.1 Understand the concept of a ratio and use ratio language to describe a ratio relationship between two quantities. *For example, "The ratio of wings to beaks in the bird house at the zoo was 2:1, because for every 2 wings there was 1 beak." "For every vote candidate A received, candidate C received nearly three votes."*

For **questions 1 to 4**, use the following information to identify the given ratios.

4 tigers, 5 bears, 3 cheetahs, and 7 lions were housed at the local zoo.

1. What is the ratio of bears to lions?

2. What is the ratio of tigers to cheetahs?

3. What is the ratio of lions to all the animals housed at the zoo?

4. Is the ratio of bears and cheetahs to all the animals a part to part ratio or a part to whole ratio?

5. On a spelling test, Gladys correctly spelled 18 of the 25 words. What is the ratio of misspelled words to all the words on the test?

(Answers are on pages 226–227.)

Rates

Rates are a special type of ratio where the two terms are different units. Rates are usually discussed in the same sentence as ratios. However, rates and ratios are different.

Ratios usually describe how much of something you have. They typically compare items using the same unit.

In contrast, rates compare one unit to some other unit. Examples of rates include pages read per hour, cost per dozen, and miles per hour. On the Smarter Balanced Assessment, you will be asked to multiply or divide an initial rate to answer various real-world problems.

Example: Franco read 40 pages of his favorite book in 3 hours. At that rate, how many pages will he read in 9 hours?

Solution: 120 pages. One way to figure out the solution is by using a multiplier or divisor. The problem states that Franco read 40 pages in 3 hours. To answer the question, 3 hours must be increased to 9 hours. The hours increase by a scale factor, or multiplier, of 3. To find out how many pages Franco reads in 9 hours, use the same scale factor.

$$40 \times 3 = 120$$

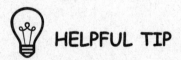 **HELPFUL TIP**

When comparing two rates, always multiply or divide to find the scale factor. Never add or subtract.

Proportions can be used to solve rate problems. A **proportion** sets two ratios equal to each other. The unit in the numerator of the first ratio must be the same as the unit in the numerator of the second ratio. The same applies to the denominators. The unit in the first ratio must be the same as the unit in the second ratio.

Example: The Parker family took 6 hours to drive 330 miles. If they drove at a constant rate, how far did they travel in 2 hours?

Solution: 110 miles. Use a proportion to solve this rate problem. Make sure that when you set up the proportion, units in one ratio must line up with the units in the second ratio. You can use cross multiplication and division to solve a proportion. Cross multiply and then divide.

$$\frac{m}{2 \text{ hours}} = \frac{330 \text{ miles}}{6 \text{ hours}}$$

$$6m = 330 \times 2$$

$$6m = 660$$

$$\frac{6m}{6} = \frac{660}{6}$$

$$m = 110$$

Practice Exercises—Rates

Common Core Standard 6.RP.A.2 Understand the concept of a unit rate a/b associated with a ratio a:b with b ≠ 0, and use rate language in the context of a ratio relationship. *For example, "This recipe has a ratio of 3 cups of flour to 4 cups of sugar, so there is 3/4 cup of flour for each cup of sugar." "We paid $75 for 15 hamburgers, which is a rate of $5 per hamburger."*

1. Paul ate 3 hot dogs in 15 minutes. At that rate, how many hot dogs will he eat in an hour and a half?

2. Preston can type 50 words per minute. If he types at the same rate, how many words can he type in 24 minutes?

3. Ronald takes 8 minutes to run 4 times around the school's track. At that rate, how long will it take him to run 6 times around the track?

4. If Jade and Holly use 72 pieces to build every model airplane, how many pieces will they use to build 6 model airplanes?

5. Joshua made 56 baskets in 6 minutes. At that rate, how many baskets did he make in 1.5 minutes?

(Answers are on page 227.)

Unit Rate and Unit Price

A **unit rate** is a specific type of ratio. It compares several of a unit to one whole of another unit. Unit rates, like all other rates, compare different units. However in unit rates, the second unit must have a quantity of 1. Unit rates can be found everywhere. The speed of an automobile is measured in miles per hour. A tree's growth is measured in feet per year. A basketball player's average is measured in points per game. These are just a few ways that you see unit rates in everyday life.

 **HELPFUL TIP**

When converting a rate into a unit rate, divide the top and bottom of the fraction by the denominator. The denominator of any unit rate must always equal 1.

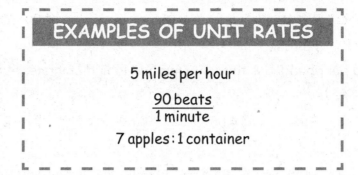

EXAMPLES OF UNIT RATES

5 miles per hour

$$\frac{90 \text{ beats}}{1 \text{ minute}}$$

7 apples : 1 container

Unit rates are usually identified by the word "per." In the box, the first unit rate is per hour, the second is per minute, and the third is per container.

Example: Trina's pet German Shepard gained 24 pounds in 6 weeks. Write the unit rate of pounds gained per week.

Solution: $\dfrac{4 \text{ pounds}}{1 \text{ week}}$ You could first write the initial rate as a comparison using division.

$$\frac{24 \text{ pounds}}{6 \text{ weeks}}$$

To find the unit rate, divide both numbers by the denominator of 6.

$$\frac{24 \text{ pounds}}{6 \text{ weeks}} \div \frac{6}{6} = \frac{4 \text{ pounds}}{1 \text{ week}}$$

The **unit price** is used to find the cost of one item. When finding the unit price, you will follow the same steps you used to find the unit rate. Unit price is written as a price per one unit.

EXAMPLES OF UNIT PRICE

$$\frac{\$1.50}{\text{lb}}$$

$0.95 per pencil

$85.00 per tire

Example: The local market sells a 5-pound bag of apples for $4.00. What is the unit price per pound?

Solution: $0.80 per pound. Use the same method to find unit rates as you use to find the unit price.

$$\frac{\$4.00}{5\ lb} \div \frac{5}{5} = \frac{\$0.80}{1\ lb}$$

Remember to divide both the top and bottom numbers of your rate by the denominator.

Example: An 8-ounce drink costs $2.25, and a 10-ounce drink costs $2.88. Which drink is the better buy? Explain your reasoning.

Solution: The 8-ounce drink is the better buy. It costs $0.28 per ounce, and the 10-ounce drink costs $0.29 per ounce.

$$\frac{\$2.25}{8\ ounces} \div \frac{8}{8} = \frac{\$0.281}{1\ ounce} = \frac{\$0.28}{1\ ounce}$$

$$\frac{\$2.88}{10\ ounces} \div \frac{10}{10} = \frac{\$0.288}{1\ ounce} = \frac{\$0.29}{1\ ounce}$$

The 10-ounce drink is rounded up to the nearest cent. The 8-ounce drink is rounded down to the nearest cent.

Practice Exercises—Unit Rate and Unit Price

Common Core Standard 6.RP.A.3.B Solve unit rate problems including those involving unit pricing and constant speed. *For example, if it took 7 hours to mow 4 lawns, then at that rate, how many lawns could be mowed in 35 hours? At what rate were lawns being mowed?*

1. Ricardo read 96 pages in 3 nights. What is the unit rate of pages he read per night?

2. Penny paid $4.00 for 5 pounds of grapes. Check all the rates that are equivalent to the rate Penny paid.

	$0.45 for 1 pound of grapes
	$12.00 for 15 pounds of grapes
	$16.00 for 18 pounds of grapes
	$2.00 for $2\frac{1}{2}$ pounds of grapes
	$0.80 for 1 pound of grapes

3. Madeline earns $32.50 for every 5 hours of baby-sitting that she does. At this rate, how much will she earn for 11 hours of baby-sitting?

4. Jan bought 6 candles for $42. What is the cost per candle?

5. Warren watched 18 movies in 6 months. What is the unit rate of movies he watched per month?

(Answers are on pages 227–229.)

Tables of Equivalent Ratios

On the Smarter Balanced Assessment, you will fill in a ratio table with missing values. There are different ways that you can complete your table. Here is a ratio table that identifies the ratio of pages read to minutes.

Pages Read	5 × 4	10		20	
Minutes	20		60	80 ÷ 4	100

When you complete any ratio table, you will need to find the multiplier or divisor that will get you from one value to another. In this table of values, 5 × 4 = 20 and 20 × 4 = 80. As you try to find the missing value for minutes, multiply the pages read by 4. If you try and find the missing values for pages read, divide the minutes by 4.

💡 **HELPFUL TIP**

After you have found the missing values in a ratio table, cross products will validate your solutions. In the previous table, you can use cross multiplication to see if the ratios are equivalent. The missing value for minutes is 40. Cross multiply the first column and the second column: 40 × 5 and 20 × 10. Since they both multiply to 200, you know that you have the correct missing value. You can perform cross multiplication anywhere in your table. If the cross products are equivalent, you have found the correct missing values.

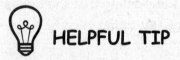

Another way to check if you have completed your equivalent ratio table correctly is by simplifying.

Example: The ratio of birds to cats is 4:1. Complete the ratio table below.

Birds	Cats
4	1
12	
20	5
	7

Solution:

Birds	Cats
4	1
12	3
20	5
28	**7**

Since there are 4 birds for every 1 cat, you can divide the birds by 4 to get the number of cats. You can also multiply the cats by 4 to get the number of birds. There are four different ratios of birds to cats (4:1, 12:3, 20:5, and 28:7). Check to see if they are all equivalent.

12:3 is reduced by the GCF of 3 and is equal to 4:1.

20:5 is reduced by the GCF of 5 and is equal to 4:1.

28:7 is reduced by the GCF of 7 and is equal to 4:1.

If each ratio is equivalent after simplifying to lowest terms, you have found the correct missing values in your table.

 **HELPFUL TIP**

Use the same process of simplifying fractions to reduce ratios to lowest terms. Divide the numerator and denominator by the greatest common factor to simplify to lowest terms.

Practice Exercises—Tables of Equivalent Ratios

Common Core Standard 6.RP.A.3.A Make tables of equivalent ratios relating quantities with whole-number measurements, find missing values in the tables, and plot the pairs of values on the coordinate plane. Use tables to compare ratios.

1. The ratio of boys to girls in Valley Middle School's Associated Student Body is 2:3. Use that information to complete the ratio table below.

Boys	Girls
	3
4	
6	9
8	
14	21

2. Complete the table of equivalent ratios below.

7	56
9	
11	88
13	104

3. Complete the table of equivalent ratios below.

Number of Apps	Total Cost
3	$4.50
6	
9	$13.50
12	
20	$30.00

4. Fill in the ratio table below.

Number of hours	2	6	8	12	20
Number of miles	14		56		

(Answers are on pages 229–230.)

Graphing Ratios

Another way to represent equivalent ratios shown in a table is with a graph.

Example: The Ocean Whale Watching Company can carry up to 150 passengers on its daily excursion. The table below shows the maximum passenger capacity for different numbers of trips.

Number of Daily Excursions	2	4	5	7	8	10
Maximum # of Passengers	300	600	750	1,050	?	1,500

Use the grid below to graph the values shown in the table. Find the maximum passenger capacity for 8 excursions, and plot that point.

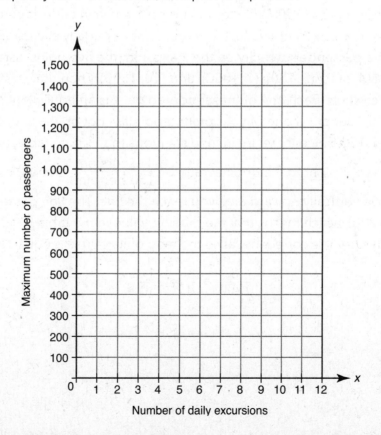

Solution:

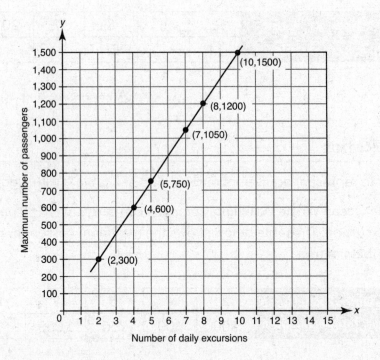

The maximum capacity for 8 excursions is 1,200 passengers. This value can be found by multiplying 8 × 150. When graphing points from a table, identify the x- and y-values for each comparison. Place the number of daily excursions on the x-axis. Place the passenger capacity on the y-axis. Plot the five points listed in the table: (2, 300); (4, 600); (5, 750); (7, 1050); and (10, 1500). Then draw a straight line through all five points. Each one of these ordered pairs is an equivalent ratio to 1 excursion to 150 people. If one of your plotted points is not on the line, it is not equivalent to 1:150. Since there are infinite solutions to this ratio table, any point on the line is also equivalent to the original ratio of $\frac{1\text{ excursion}}{150\text{ people}}$. Along the x-axis, go to 8. Then move vertically upward until you reach the line. The line passes through the point (8, 1200), which means that the missing value in the table is 1,200. You can confirm that this point is correct because the ratio of its values is equal to 1:150.

$$\frac{8}{1200} \div \frac{8}{8} = \frac{1}{150}$$

Practice Exercises—Graphing Ratios

Common Core Standard 6.RP.A.3.A Make tables of equivalent ratios relating quantities with whole-number measurements, find missing values in the tables, and plot the pairs of values on the coordinate plane. Use tables to compare ratios.

1. Trina and Michael went to the store to buy their favorite assorted candies. The treats are sold at a unit price of $2.50 per pound.

   Part A: Complete the table below.

Candy (lb)	Price per Pound
1	$2.50
2	$5.00
3	
4	$10.00

   Part B: Graph the values from the table.

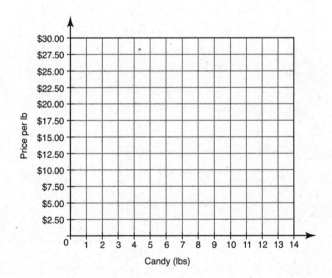

   Part C: How much would the children pay if they purchased 9 pounds of candy?

2. Brenda takes 6 hours to make 1 coffee table.

Part A: Use Brenda's rate to complete the ratio table below.

Number of Coffee Tables	1	2		7
Time (hours)	6		24	

Part B: Identify the four ordered pairs in the table (coffee tables, hours).

Part C: Graph the ordered pairs on the coordinate plane.

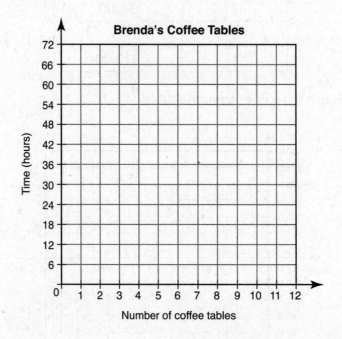

(Answers are on pages 230–232.)

Percent

Percent is another way that you can write a ratio. The word *percent* means "out of 100." The symbol % is used to represent the word percent. For example, 40% can be looked at as 40 out of 100. A percent is always a part to whole ratio since every percent is out of 100. You can say that 12 out of 100 is equivalent to 12%. On the SBAC Assessment, you will solve different types of percent problems. You might be asked to find the percent of a number.

Example: 30% of the 200 students at Marion Academy earned a 3.5 or higher GPA on their semester grades. How many students earned a GPA of 3.5 or above?

Solution: 60. One way to find the solution is to use a diagram of a one hundred square grid. Since you are trying to find 30% out of 200, you will need two grids. As shown in the diagram, 30 of the 100 squares in each grid are shaded.

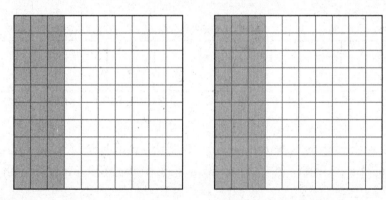

The solution is 60 because there are 60 squares shaded out of the 200 total squares.

Another way to find the percent of a number is by using multiplication. The word "of" in percent problems means to multiply. You can change the percent into a decimal and multiply, or you can change the percent into a fraction and multiply.

Example: 30% of all the trees in Yorba Regional Park are palm trees. If there are 400 trees in the park, how many are palm trees?

Solution: 120. You can solve this problem using several different methods. The first multiplies fractions. Just remember to multiply across the numerators and the denominators. Start by changing the percent to a fraction.

$$30\% = \frac{30}{100}$$

$$\frac{30}{100} \times \frac{400}{1} = \frac{12,000}{100}$$

After multiplying, divide 12,000 by 100 to get 120.

The second method multiplies decimals. First change 30% to 0.3 because 30% is equal to thirty hundredths (0.30) or three-tenths (0.3). Then multiply 0.3 × 400.

$$
\begin{array}{r}
400 \\
\times\ 0.3 \\
\hline
120\ 0
\end{array}
$$

There is one digit after the decimal point in the first number. There is no decimal in the second factor. Therefore, there will be one digit after the decimal point in your product. Start at the end of 1,200 and move your decimal one place to the left.

The third method uses a **tape diagram.** This is a visual that uses rectangular boxes to represent parts of a ratio. A tape diagram is another visual model that can be used to represent ratios and percent. (See the illustration below.)

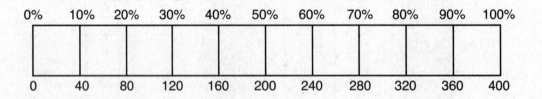

0%	10%	20%	30%	40%	50%	60%	70%	80%	90%	100%
0	40	80	120	160	200	240	280	320	360	400

The tape diagram shows that for every 10%, the number of trees increases by 40. The solution to the problem is 120 because 30% of the 400 lines up with 120.

 **HELPFUL TIP**

When you take 10% of any number, just move the decimal point one place to the left in that number: 10% of 83.2 = 8.32. When finding 40% of 83.2, multiply 8.32 (which is 10%) by 4.

Another type of percent problem you will solve on the SBAC Assessment is a part to part ratio.

Example: By halftime, Ronnie and Peter had eaten a combined 30 pieces of shrimp at a football party. This represented 60% of the entire bowl of shrimp. How many shrimp were in the bowl at the start of the game?

Solution: 50. This problem can be solved using several different methods. In the first, you write an equation. Let s equal the number of shrimp at the start of the game.

$$0.60s = 30$$

Divide both sides by 0.6 or 0.60.

$$\frac{\cancel{0.60}s}{\cancel{0.60}} = \frac{30}{0.60}$$

$$s = 50$$

You can instead use a tape diagram to solve the problem.

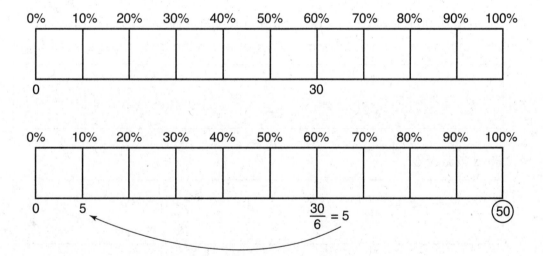

When solving a part to part percent problem, place the given number directly under the given percent. The number 30 will be placed directly under the 60%. Divide 30 by 6 because you are trying to find out what 10% is equal to. Since 10% = 5 and you are trying to find the total, multiply 5 × 10 = 50. If 10% = 5, then 100% = 50.

Practice Exercises—Percent

> **Common Core Standard 6.RP.A.3.C** Find a percent of a quantity as a rate per 100 (e.g., 30% of a quantity means 30/100 times the quantity); solve problems involving finding the whole, given a part and the percent.

1. 100% of _____ is 40.

2. Raul made 16 out of 20 free throws at his basketball tournament. What percent of free throws did he miss?

3. Brian read 80 pages of his book during his winter break. This represented 25% of the entire book. How many pages are in the book that he is reading?

4. Find 12% of 67.

5. Convert $\frac{7}{8}$ to a percent.

(Answers are on pages 232–233.)

Measurement Conversions

In fifth grade, you converted measurement units within given measurement systems. For example, you might have converted 8 cups to 4 pints, 64 ounces to 4 pounds, or even 5 m to 500 cm.

2 cups	1 pint
16 ounces	1 pound
100 centimeters	1 meter

You will use this knowledge to help you with the types of conversions that Smarter Balanced has created for you. In Grade 6, the intent of the Common Core is to convert units by using ratios.

Example:

Part A: Given 1 inch = 2.54 centimeters, enter the value that will complete this expression for converting 2 feet to centimeters.

$$\left(\frac{2\,\text{feet}}{1}\right) \times \frac{\boxed{}}{1\,\text{foot}} \times \left(\frac{2.54\,\text{centimeters}}{1\,\text{inch}}\right)$$

Part B: How many centimeters are in 2 feet?

Solution:

Part A: 12 inches. For this part of the problem, you just need to identify how many inches are in a foot. The unit for the numerator of the second ratio must match the unit for the denominator in the third ratio (inches).

Part B: 60.96 centimeters. Use the following steps to find the solution.

1. First write the initial rate as a fraction. To write any number as a fraction, place that value over 1: $\left(\frac{2\,\text{feet}}{1}\right)$.

2. The denominator of the second rate *must* include the same unit as the numerator in the first rate. In this problem, that unit is feet.

3. The unit for the numerator in the second ratio must match the unit for the denominator in the third ratio (inches). You are given that 2.54 centimeters = 1 inch in the third ratio. So 12 inches will be inserted as the numerator of the second ratio.

4. Cross reduce the units so that the unit you are looking for is the only one remaining (centimeters).

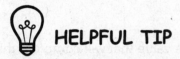

$$\left(\frac{2\ \cancel{feet}}{\cancel{1}}\right) \times \frac{\boxed{}}{1\ \cancel{foot}} \times \left(\frac{2.54\ \text{centimeters}}{1\ \cancel{inch}}\right)$$

5. Multiply across the top and the bottom to get your numerical answer:

$$2 \times 12 \times 2.54 = 60.96\ \text{centimeters}$$

💡 **HELPFUL TIP**

The denominator's unit in the second ratio must match the numerator's unit in the first ratio. This way you can reduce, or cancel out, the units. The same rule applies to the second and third ratios.

Many measurements in our world can be converted. You will need to know some basic conversions to solve the types of questions on the SBAC Assessment. (See the table below.)

12 inches	1 foot
16 ounces	1 pound
4 quarts	1 gallon
2 cups	1 pint
3 feet	1 yard
2,000 pounds	1 ton
2.54 cm	1 inch
8 fluid ounces	1 cup

Practice Exercises—Measurement Conversions

> **Common Core Standard 6.RP.A.3.D** Use ratio reasoning to convert measurement units; manipulate and transform units appropriately when multiplying or dividing quantities.

1. 96 ounces = _____ lb

2. 30 inches = _____ ft

3. Enter the value that will complete this expression for converting 6.5 yards to inches.

$$\left(\frac{6.5\,\text{yards}}{1}\right) \times \left(\frac{\boxed{}\,\text{feet}}{1\,\text{yard}}\right) \times \left(\frac{12\,\text{inches}}{1\,\text{foot}}\right)$$

4. Enter the value that will complete the expression for converting 5 pounds to ounces.

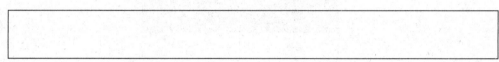

$$\left(\frac{5\,\text{pounds}}{1}\right) \times \left(\frac{\boxed{}\,\text{ounces}}{1\,\text{pound}}\right)$$

5. 10 quarts = _____ gallons

(Answers are on page 233.)

PRACTICE REVIEW TEST:
Ratios and Proportional Thinking

1. 16 is _____% of 20.

2. The table below represents a proportional relationship. Complete the table by filling in the missing values.

x	y
3	9
5	
7	21
	27

3. 71 is 50% of what number?

4. Convert $\frac{5}{8}$ to a percent.

5. The Jonas Dry Cleaning Store cleans an average of 120 shirts every 5 hours. At this rate, how long would it take to clean 300 shirts?

6. 12 students in the math club solved 126 problems in 7 hours. What is the unit rate of problems solved per hour?

7. Logan reads at a constant rate of 8 pages in 20 minutes. Complete the table for Logan's reading rate.

Number of Pages		8		48
Number of Minutes	10		60	

8. A 12-ounce can of soda costs $1.62, and a 16-ounce can of soda costs $2.08. Which can of soda is the better buy? Explain your reasoning.

9. The Martinez family went to dinner on Thursday night. The cost of the dinner was $72.00. If they left a 15% tip, what was the amount of the tip?

10. Find 30% of 124.

11. Movie tickets cost $12 each. Complete the table of equivalent ratios.

Tickets	1		3	
Total Cost	12	24		48

12. Dominique has 2 cats and 3 dogs. Place a check next to the box if the ratio identifies dogs to cats.

	2 + 3
	3 to 2
	2:3
	$\frac{3}{2}$
	3 − 2
	3:2

13. 89 is 100% of what number?

14. The ratio of spoons to forks in Martha's kitchen drawer is 3 to 4. If there are 20 forks in the kitchen drawer, how many spoons are there?

15. Check all the expressions that are equivalent to 45% of 320.

A. _____ 0.45 × 32.0

B. _____ 4.5 × 320

C. _____ 0.45 × 320

D. _____ $\frac{45}{100}$ × 320

16. Fernando walked 6 miles in 4 hours. At this rate, how many miles will he walk in 10 hours?

17. Christine surveyed the students in her class to find out their favorite dessert. What percent of Christine's classmates did *not* choose ice cream as their favorite dessert?

Dessert	Number
Pie	7
Cupcakes	10
Ice cream	8
Cookies	15

Percent:

18. Use the following shapes to identify the given ratios.

A. Identify the ratio of rectangles to triangles.

B. Identify the ratio of circles and rectangles to all the shapes.

C. Is the ratio of triangles to all the shapes a part to part or a part to whole ratio?

19. Enter the values that will complete this expression for converting 3.5 yards to inches.

$$\left(\frac{3.5 \text{ yards}}{1}\right) \times \left(\frac{\boxed{} \text{ feet}}{\boxed{} \text{ yards}}\right) \times \left(\frac{12 \text{ inches}}{1 \text{ foot}}\right) = \underline{\hspace{1cm}} \text{ inches}$$

Feet:

Yards:

Inches:

20. **Part A:** Graph the following ratio table.

Hours Worked	$ Earned
15	135
20	180
25	225
30	270

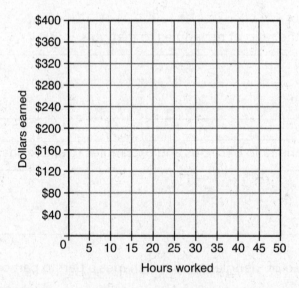

Part B: Use the graph to find out how many hours you would need to work to earn $360.

21. A water pump can pump 325 gallons from a pool in 10 minutes. What is the unit rate of the pump in gallons per minute?

(Answers are on pages 234–237.)

Expressions and Equations

In this chapter, you will be working on applying your prior knowledge of basic arithmetic facts to algebraic expressions. You will be writing expressions from words and evaluating those expressions once you identify any missing values. You will then explore other ways to write the same expressions by using different properties of operations. You will use two equivalent expressions to form an equation. Finally, you will write and solve one-step equations and inequalities.

Exponents

Numerical expressions, such as 3 + 2 or 9 × 8, can be solved by either adding or multiplying the two numbers together. Another type of numerical expression that can be solved is 3^4. The 3 in the expression is called the **base**. The base is the number that is going to be raised to a power or the number that is being multiplied. The 4 in the expression is called either the **exponent** or the **power**. The exponent is the number above and to the right of the base. The exponent identifies how many times you multiply the base times itself. A great way to solve a power is by first **expanding** the power. To do this, break up the expression by showing the repeated multiplication.

$$3^4 \text{ (Exponential Power)}$$

$$3 \times 3 \times 3 \times 3 \text{ (Expanded Form)}$$

$$81 \text{ (Standard Form Solution)}$$

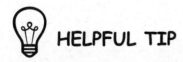 **HELPFUL TIP**

Sometimes rewriting the expression will help to simplify the multiplication!

$$3^4$$

$$3 \times 3 \times 3 \times 3$$

$$9 \times 9$$

$$81$$

Make sure you don't make common mistakes. For instance, do not think that 3^4 is the same as multiplying 3×4, which is equivalent to 12. Do not rewrite 3^4 as $4 \times 4 \times 4$, which equals 64. Remember that 3^4 is $3 \times 3 \times 3 \times 3$, which equals 81.

Variables are letters that take the place of a number. Variables can also be written with exponential powers. For example, when you are trying to find the area of a square, you multiply one side by another side (side $\times$ side). Since both sides are equivalent, you could identify the area of a square with the expression s^2, where s equals the length of one side. The volume of a cube is found by multiplying side $\times$ side $\times$ side. Since all the sides are identical, you could find the volume of a cube by using the expression s^3, where s equals the length of one side.

The surface area of a cube can be found by solving the expression $6s^2$. A cube has six sides. All the sides are squares. The area of each side is found by multiplying side $\times$ side. To find the surface area of the entire cube, multiply the area of one side by 6.

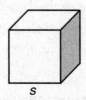

s

HOW TO READ EXPONENTS

Read the base and then the exponent. An exponent of 2 is said to be squared. An exponent of 3 is said to be cubed.

> 5^6 is read as "five to the sixth power."
> 9^{10} is read as "nine to the tenth power."
> 7^2 is read as "seven to the second power" or as "seven squared."
> 4^3 is read as "four to the third power" or as "four cubed."

Example: Evaluate: 4^3

Solution: 64. 4^3 is equivalent to $4 \times 4 \times 4 = 16 \times 4 = 64$.

Example: Select all the expressions below that are equivalent to 3^6. Circle all that apply.

A. $3 \times 3 \times 3 \times 3 \times 3$

B. 6×3

C. $6 \times 6 \times 6$

D. $3 \times 3 \times 3 \times 3 \times 3 \times 3$

E. $9 \times 9 \times 9$

Solution: D and E. The expression $3^6 = 3 \times 3 \times 3 \times 3 \times 3 \times 3$. Each 3×3 can be grouped together to form 9. So the value of 3^6 is also equivalent to the value of $9 \times 9 \times 9$.

Practice Exercises—Exponents

Common Core Standard 6.EE.A.1 Write and evaluate numerical expressions involving whole-number exponents.

Questions 1-3: Write each exponential power in expanded form and solve, if possible.

1. 2^5

2. n^3

3. 1.5^6

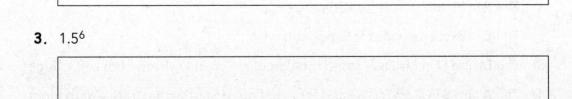

4. Tabitha thinks that 2^4 is equivalent to 8. She reasons that four 2s add up to 8. Identify the flaw in Tabitha's reasoning.

5. Select all the expressions below that are equivalent to 5^4. Circle all that apply.

   A. $4 \times 4 \times 4 \times 4 \times 4$

   B. 625

   C. 5×4

   D. $5 \times 5 \times 5 \times 5$

   E. $5 \times 25 \times 5$

(Answers are on page 237.)

Order of Operations

In math, we follow a specific order when solving any problem where there is more than one operation. This specific order is called the **order of operations**. Originally written to help solve polynomials in algebra, this specific order of operations has been used for close to 400 years.

STEP 1   Perform any operations inside of grouping symbols.

STEP 2   Perform any exponential powers.

STEP 3   Multiply or divide from left to right.

STEP 4   Add or subtract from left to right.

Since parentheses are the main grouping symbol you will deal with, a catchy phrase was created to help students remember the order. The saying is, "Please Excuse My Dear Aunt Sally."

1. The **P** in Please stands for Parentheses.

2. The **E** in Excuse stands for Exponents.

3. The **M** and **D** in My Dear stand for Multiplication or Division from Left to Right.

4. The **A** and **S** in Aunt Sally stand for Addition or Subtraction from Left to Right.

IMPORTANT TIPS TO SOLVING ORDER OF OPERATION PROBLEMS

1. When there is more than one operation in the grouping symbol, follow the standard order of operations.

2. When there is multiplication or division in the same problem, the order doesn't matter. Solve them from left to right even if the division is written first.

3. When there is addition or subtraction in the same problem, the order doesn't matter. Solve them from left to right even if the subtraction is written first.

4. When there are operations above and below a division bar, it is best to solve everything in the numerator first. Then solve everything in the denominator. Afterward, divide the top number by the bottom number.

Practice Exercises—Order of Operations

Common Core Standard 6.EE.A.1 Write and solve numerical expressions involving whole-number exponents.

1. $17 + 3^2 - 5 \times 4$

2. $83 - 24 \div 6 + (5^2 + 9)$

3. $27 + 18 \div 3$

4. $15 + 3^3 - 30 \div 10$

5. $9^2 - 21 \div 7 \times (5 + 8)$

(Answers are on page 237.)

Identifying Parts of an Expression

Students will be asked to identify parts of an **algebraic or numerical expression**. An expression is a mathematical phrase that contains terms and has no equals sign. First you need to understand the mathematical vocabulary behind them. **Terms** are numbers and/or variables that are separated by an addition (+) or a subtraction (−) sign. Terms are an integral part of every expression.

Example: Identify the number of terms in the expression: $3x + 12y + 17$.

Solution: 3. There are three terms, $3x$ and $12y$ and 17. They are separated by two plus signs in the expression.

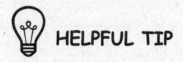 **HELPFUL TIP**

The number of terms is *always* one more than the number of plus (+) and minus (−) signs in the expression.

In the previous example, $3x$ and $12y$ are both **variable terms**. In other words, these terms contain a letter (a variable) that takes the place of a number. In $3x$, 3 is the **coefficient**, which is the number in front of the variable x. In $12y$, 12 is the coefficient of the variable y. In $3x$, the 3 represents how many groups of x you have. For instance, if the value of x is 7, you would have 3 groups of 7, which would be equivalent to 21.

In the previous example, the number 17 is a **numerical term** because it is simply a number. The 17 is also called a **constant** because it is a numerical term that will not change.

Example: Use the following expression to complete the table.

$$7x + 9y + 4z + 8$$

Expression	Number of Terms	Constant Term(s)	Term(s) with Variables	Coefficient(s) of the Variable(s)
$7x + 9y + 4z + 8$				

Solution:

Expression	Number of Terms	Constant Term(s)	Term(s) with Variables	Coefficient(s) of the Variable(s)
$7x + 9y + 4z + 8$	4	8	$7x, 9y, 4z$	7, 9, 4

There are four terms because the expression has three plus or minus signs in it. The number that will stay the same is 8. It is the constant. There are three variable terms. They each contain a letter, or variable. The coefficients are the numbers in front of each variable (7, 9, and 4).

Practice Exercises—Identifying Parts of an Expression

Common Core Standard 6.EE.A.2.B Identify parts of an expression using mathematical terms (sum, term, product, factor, quotient, coefficient); view one or more parts of an expression as a single entity. *For example, describe the expression 2(8 + 7) as a product of two factors; view (8 + 7) as both a single entity and a sum of two terms.*

1. Identify the number of terms, the coefficients, and the constants in the following table.

	Number of Terms	Coefficient(s)	Constant(s)
$5x + 7$			
$0.5x - 12$			
$2x + 6 - 3y$			

2. In the expression $4x + 12y + 18$, which term is the constant?

3. In the expression $12xyz + 44n$, how many terms are present?

4. Consider the expression $15 + 9y - 60$.

   Identify the coefficient(s) in the expression.

(Answers are on page 238.)

Writing and Solving Expressions

When writing an expression, key words help to identify the operation. The following table shows some key words that will help you identify which operation to use. Although there are many more key words, the table will help to write expressions from words.

Addition	Subtraction	Multiplication	Division
Sum	Difference	Product	Quotient
More than	Less than	Times	Split
Add	Decrease	Groups of	Cut
Increase	Minus	Factor	Into

 SBAC HINT

On the Smarter Balanced Assessment, you might be asked to write an expression that includes variables or numerical values. The following two examples show you what that type of question might look like on the actual assessment and acceptable answers.

Example: Write the following variable expression from words:

The product of 12 and a number

Solution: $12x$. The expression $12x$ shows the multiplication of 12 and a number, x.

Example: Tanya spent $45 out of the $160 she received for graduation. Write an expression to identify how much money she has left.

Solution: $160 - 45$. The expression $160 - 45$ identifies the difference between what Tanya started with and what she spent.

Variable expressions are expressions that contain a variable. They can be solved only when a value is given to represent the variable. For example, $12x$ is a variable expression that cannot be solved as written. However, if you are given a value for x, the expression can be solved. If $x = 9$, substitute the x with 9 and solve the expression.

$$12x$$

$$12(9)$$

$$12 \times 9$$

$$108$$

Numerical expressions are expressions that contain only numbers. They can be solved because there are no variables. In the previous example, the numerical expression $160 - 45$ can be solved. Tanya has $115 left.

Students will also be asked to solve variable expressions when the value of the variable is given. Substitute the value of the variable into the expression to solve.

Example: Evaluate $6n$ when $n = 8$.

Solution: 48. Substitute 8 for the variable n and then multiply. The product is $6(8) = 48$. Remember that when you substitute a number for a variable and that substituted number is next to another number, you must put the substitute into parentheses. In this example, $6n$ represents 6 groups of n. If you don't put the 8 into parentheses, your solution will be 68, which is incorrect.

Practice Exercises—Writing and Solving Expressions

Common Core Standard 6.EE.A.2.A Write expressions that record operations with numbers and with letters standing for numbers. *For example, express the calculation "Subtract y from 5" as 5 – y.*

Common Core Standard 6.EE.A.2.C Evaluate expressions at specific values of their variables. Include expressions that arise from formulas used in real-world problems. Perform arithmetic operations, including those involving whole-number exponents, in the conventional order when there are no parentheses to specify a particular order (Order of Operations). *For example, use the formulas $V = s^3$ and $A = 6s^2$ to find the volume and surface area of a cube with sides of length s = 1/2.*

Write the following expressions from words.

1. The difference of a number and nine

2. Twice the sum of six and a number

3. The product of four and a number

4. Solve the following expression when $x = 4$, $y = \dfrac{1}{2}$, and $z = 9$.

$12y - x$

5. Solve the expression $12c$ when $c = 9$.

(Answers are on page 238.)

Distributive Property and Equivalent Expressions

Another target of sixth-grade math is to identify equivalent expressions. Students will simplify expressions in a variety of ways.

Some expressions will require you to combine **like terms**. These are terms that all include the same variable raised to the same power.

Example: Simplify $x + x + x$.

Solution: $3x$. In this example, all three x-terms are to the first power. So they are like terms. Therefore, you can combine or add the terms together.

Example: Simplify the expression $5x + 7 - 3x$.

Solution: $2x + 7$. The x-terms can be combined because they are both to the same power (the first power). This means that there is no exponent above each x. *You cannot combine variable terms and constant terms.*

Equivalent expressions can also be written by **factoring**. When factoring, you divide out the greatest common factor for each term.

Example: Factor out the GCF (greatest common factor) for the expression $4x + 8$.

Solution: $4(x + 2)$. The greatest number that goes into both terms is 4. Divide both terms by 4 to get the solution.

$$\frac{4x}{4} + \frac{8}{4}$$
$$1x + 2$$

You are still left with the 4 that you divided out.

$$4(x + 2)$$

There are many other equivalent expressions to $4x + 8$. Some of these include but are not limited to $2x + 2x + 8$, $3x + x + 6 + 2$, and $2(2x + 4)$. There are infinite amounts of equivalent expressions. However, on the assessment, you will probably be asked to factor out the GCF (greatest common factor). So in that case, only $4(x + 2)$ would be an acceptable answer.

Equivalent expressions do not have to include only variables. The numerical expression $32 + 40$ could also be factored using the GCF.

Example: Simplify the expression 32 + 40 by factoring out the greatest common factor.

Solution: 8(4 + 5). The GCF is 8.

$$\frac{32}{8} + \frac{40}{8}$$
$$4 + 5$$

You are still left with the 8 that you divided out.

$$8(4 + 5)$$

Students can check to see if they factored out the GCF correctly by using the **distributive property**. To use the distributive property, simply multiply the number in front of the parentheses by each term inside the parentheses. If the expression inside the parentheses contains a minus sign (−), make sure to include that when multiplying.

$$8 \times 4 = 32 \text{ and } 8 \times 5 = 40$$

Using the order of operations can help prove why and how the distributive property works.

$$8(4 + 5)$$
$$8(9)$$
$$72$$

Now let's see how the distributive property works.

$$8(4 + 5)$$
$$8(4) + 8(5)$$
$$32 + 40$$
$$72$$

Example: Use the distributive property to simplify the expression $7(3x + 4y)$.

Solution: $21x + 28y$. Multiply 7 by both terms inside of the parentheses. Remember that you *cannot* combine the x- and y-terms because they are different variable terms.

$$7(3x + 4y)$$
$$7(3x) + 7(4y)$$
$$21x + 28y$$

Practice Exercises—Distributive Property and Equivalent Expressions

> **Common Core Standard 6.EE.A.3** Apply the properties of operations to generate equivalent expressions. *For example, apply the distributive property to the expression 3(2 + x) to produce the equivalent expression 6 + 3x; apply the distributive property to the expression 24x + 18y to produce the equivalent expression 6(4x + 3y); apply properties of operations to y + y + y to produce the equivalent expression 3y.*

1. Simplify the expression $3x + 4y - x - 9$.

2. Use the distributive property to simplify $4(2x - 5y)$.

3. Factor out the GCF to simplify $24s + 32t$.

4. Fill in the missing number: ___ $(8 + 9) = 56 + 63$

5. Select all the expressions that are equivalent to $8x + 16$. Circle the correct letter(s).

    A. $2(4x + 16)$
    B. $8(x + 2)$
    C. $4x + 4 + 12$
    D. $(2x + 4)4$
    E. $10x - 3x + x + 16$

(Answers are on pages 238–239.)

Writing and Solving Equations

Earlier in this chapter, you learned how to write expressions. Now you will use that knowledge to create algebraic equations. **Equations** combine two equivalent expressions. Equations are extremely important in sixth grade. Even though you have been solving equations for years, you will now be asked to solve them using algebraic methods.

You know that $16 - 9 = 7$ is an equation because the expression on the left side has the same value as the expression on the right side. Both expressions are equivalent to 7. Whether expressions are numerical or variable, when both sides of the equals sign have the same value, you have created an equation. For example, $3s = 21$ is an equation even though it has a variable expression on the left and a numerical expression on the right.

When you write an equation, you use the same key words as when you write an expression. Those words are listed in a table in the section "Writing and Solving Expressions" earlier in this chapter.

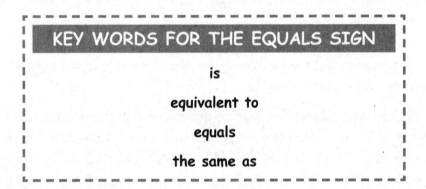

KEY WORDS FOR THE EQUALS SIGN

is

equivalent to

equals

the same as

 IMPORTANT NOTE

Be careful when looking for key words. Make sure you look at the context of the words when writing your equation. Some key words are very common, and they might have no meaning at all in the problem.

Example: Your sixth-grade physical education class has a goal of running a combined 12 miles by Friday. As of Thursday, your class has run a total of 10.5 miles. Write and solve an equation that identifies how many more miles your class needs to run to meet the goal.

Solution: There are many ways that you could write the same equation. Some of them are shown below. They all let m equal the number of miles needed to meet the goal.

- $12 = 10.5 + m$
- $m + 10.5 = 12$
- $12 - 10.5 = m$
- $12 - m = 10.5$

The four equations listed above all represent the same information. Your class has already run 10.5 miles and still needs to run an unspecified number of miles to reach 12 miles.

To solve any algebraic equation, you can use inverse operations and balancing both sides of the equation. **Inverse operations** are opposite operations. The opposite of addition is subtraction, and the opposite of multiplication is division. These inverse operations are used to **isolate** the variable. In other words, inverse operations are used to get the variable by itself on one side of the equation. Then you can find the value of the variable.

Previously, you learned that $5n$ means 5 groups of n. In the equation $5n = 20$, you are trying to find the value of n. You know that n is multiplied by 5 to reach 20. You know that 5 groups of 4 equal 20. Let's explore how you can use an inverse operation to solve this problem. In $5n = 20$, simply divide both sides by 5 to find the value of n.

 IMPORTANT NOTE

An equation starts out balanced. If it weren't balanced, there would be no equals sign (=). If you use an inverse operation on one side of the equation, *you must* perform the same inverse operation to the other side. For example, if you divide by 5 on one side of the equals sign, you must divide by 5 on the other side of the equals sign. The goal is to isolate and find the actual value of the variable while keeping the equation balanced.

Example: Solve for *n*: $5n = 20$

Solution: $n = 4$. Isolate the variable *n* by dividing both sides by 5. Since 5 is multiplied by *n*, the inverse operation is to divide 5.

$$5n = 20$$
$$\frac{5n}{5} = \frac{20}{5}$$
$$1n = 4$$
$$n = 4$$

After dividing both sides, you are left with $1n$ on the left side and with 4 on the right side. You don't need to write a coefficient of 1 in front of a variable because $1n$ is the same as *n*. The last thing you need to do is prove that the value of the variable is correct. You can do this by substituting 4 back into the original equation.

$$5(4) = 20$$
$$20 = 20$$

As you can see, 4 is the correct value because it makes the equation true!

Practice Exercises—Writing and Solving Equations

Common Core Standard 6.EE.B.5 Understand solving an equation or inequality as a process of answering a question: which values from a specified set, if any, make the equation true or inequality true? Use substitution to determine whether a given number in a specified set makes an equation or inequality true.

Common Core Standard 6.EE.B.7 Solve real-world and mathematical problems by writing and solving equations of the form $x + p = q$ and $px = q$ for cases in which *p, q,* and *x* are all nonnegative rational numbers.

1. Write and solve the following equation.

   A number divided by 12 is 10

2. Solve for x: $42.5 = 5x$

[ ]

3. Kate needs $1\frac{1}{2}$ cups of sugar to make her famous muffins. When she looked in her pantry, she saw that she had only $\frac{3}{4}$ of a cup of sugar. Write and solve an equation that identifies how much more sugar Kate will need to make her famous muffins.

[ ]

4. Check all the following equations that have 5 as a solution.

   A. $c + 13 = 19$ ____

   B. $7 \times c = 35$ ____

   C. $11c = 65$ ____

   D. $45 \div c = 9$ ____

5. Consider the following.

$$3.5n = 17.5$$

Find the value of n.

[ ]

(Answers are on page 239.)

Inequalities

In the previous section, you worked on finding values that made equations true. The equals sign (=), which is found in all equations, signifies that two expressions are equivalent. When two expressions are not equivalent, though, they are separated by an **inequality** symbol.

THE FOUR INEQUALITY SYMBOLS

> < is the "less than" symbol. It indicates that the number or expression on the left is smaller than the number or expression on the right.

> > is the "greater than" symbol. It indicates that the number or expression on the left is greater than the number or expression on the right.

> ≤ is the "less than or equal to" symbol. It indicates that the number or expression on the left is either less than or equal to the number or expression on the right.

> ≥ is the "greater than or equal to" symbol. It indicates that the number or expression on the left is either greater than or equal to the number or expression on the right.

 **SBAC HINT**

On the Smarter Balanced Assessment, you will be asked to write inequalities from words, solve one-step inequalities, and even graph the solutions to inequalities on number lines.

Let's explore the three uses of inequalities.

Writing inequalities: To write an inequality from words, use the same indicators that helped you write expressions or equations. The only difference is that you will now be writing expressions that either could be or are not equivalent to each other.

Example: To ride the extreme roller coaster, children must be at least 42 inches tall. Write an inequality that represents the height, *h*, a person must be to go on the ride.

Solution: $h \geq 42$. Anyone that is 42 inches or taller can go on the ride. The inequality identifies that *h* is equal to or greater than 42.

Example: Louis has less than 1,000 baseball cards in his collection. Write an inequality that represents how many cards, *c*, Louis could have.

Solution: $c < 1{,}000$. Any **whole number** (counting number, including zero) less than 1,000 is part of the solution set. Louis could have 327 cards or 999 cards in his collection. However, he couldn't have 1,000 or more.

Solving inequalities: When solving a one-step inequality, your goal is to find the value of the variable that makes the inequality true. Every inequality has an **infinite** number of solutions. In other words, every inequality has an endless number of numerical values that makes it true.

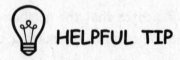 **HELPFUL TIP**

In previous equation problems, the inverse operation was used to solve for the variable. Use the inverse operation to solve one-step inequality problems as well.

Example: Solve for *x*: $3x < 27$

Solution: $x < 9$. To solve this inequality, isolate the variable just like you did when solving equations. Identify the inverse operation and use it on both sides of your inequality. The inverse operation of multiplying by 3 is dividing by 3. Make sure that you divide both sides by 3. The solution set is any number that is less than 9.

$$3x < 27$$
$$\frac{3x}{3} < \frac{27}{3}$$
$$x < 9$$

Example: Solve for t: $36.4 > t - 17.8$

Solution: $t < 54.2$. To solve the inequality, isolate the variable by adding 17.8 to both sides. The solution is $54.2 > t$, which is $t < 54.2$.

$$36.4 > t \; \cancel{-17.8}$$
$$+ 17.8 \qquad \cancel{+17.8}$$
$$54.2 > t$$

 HELPFUL TIP

When the variable is on the right side of an inequality, it is sometimes helpful to switch the two expressions. For example, $54.2 > t$ is the same as $t < 54.2$. The inequality is now read as "t is less than 54.2." When the variable is on the left side, graphing the inequality follows a specific pattern that will be shown later.

Graphing inequalities: The solution set to any inequality can be graphed on a number line. Use the following steps when graphing inequalities.

STEP 1 Identify if the solution set is less than (<), greater than (>), less than or equal to (≤), or greater than or equal to (≥) the given value.

For example, look at the inequality $x > 6$. The solution set is all numbers that are larger than 6. So 7, 10, 15, and 20 are just a few examples that make this inequality true.

STEP 2 Place an open or a closed circle on top of the number line at the value's least value (for > and ≥) or greatest value (for < or ≤) for each inequality.

- An open circle signifies that the value being graphed is *not* part of the solution set.
- A closed circle signifies that the value being graph is included in the solution set.

For example, when $x > 6$, place an open circle above the number line at 6.

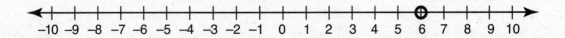

STEP 3 Draw an arrow from the open or closed circle in the direction that identifies the solution set. In $x > 6$, draw an arrow that starts at the open circle and points to the right.

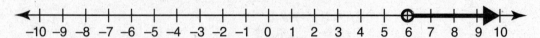

Remember that when the variable is on the left side ($x > 6$), the arrow will *always* point in the same direction as the inequality. Since the arrow is pointing to the right, the solution set is all the values that are to the right of 6 on the number line.

Example: Tanya sent more than 324 text messages over the last month.

Part A: Write an inequality that represents how many text messages Tanya sent over the last month, t.

Part B: Graph the inequality on a number line.

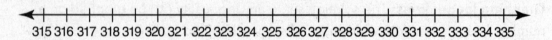

Solution:

Part A: $t > 324$. The solution set is all the numbers that are greater than 324.

Part B: The graph contains an open circle at 324 with an arrow pointing toward the right.

Example: Solve and graph the following inequality on a number line.

$$54 \leq 9c$$

Solution: $c \geq 6$. Divide both sides by 9 to solve the inequality. Then switch the order of the inequality to graph it on the number line.

$$54 \leq 9c$$

$$\frac{54}{9} \leq \frac{9c}{9}$$

$$6 \leq c \text{ or } c \geq 6$$

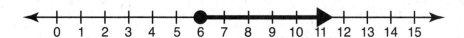

Example: Amber's parents are letting her have, at most, twenty friends at her birthday party.

Part A: Write an inequality that represents the number of friends, f, Amber can have at her party.

Part B: Graph the solution set for the number of friends that Amber can invite to her party.

Solution:

Part A: $f \leq 20$. The solution set is all the whole numbers that are equal to and less than 20.

Part B: The number 20 will have a closed circle with an arrow pointing to the left.

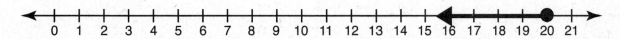

Practice Exercises—Inequalities

> **Common Core Standard 6.EE.B.5** Understand solving an equation or inequality as a process of answering a question: which values from a specified set, if any, make the equation or inequality true? Use substitution to determine whether a given number in a specified set makes an equation or inequality true.
>
> **Common Core Standard 6.EE.B.8** Write an inequality of the form $x > c$ or $x < c$ to represent a constraint or condition in a real-world or mathematical problem. Recognize that inequalities of the form $x > c$ or $x < c$ have infinitely many solutions; represent solutions of such inequalities on number line diagrams.

1. Complete the table below for the inequality $x > -3$. Check True if the number is in the solution set of the inequality. Check False if it is not.

Value of x	True	False
–4.2		
$|-7|$		
$-1\frac{1}{4}$		
–3.9		

2. Ana must earn at least \$2,500 to buy a used car. Write an inequality to represent how much money, m, Ana must make to buy the car.

3. Part A: Solve the inequality: $x - 19 > 23$

Part B: Graph the inequality on a number line.

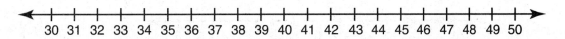

4. Complete the table below for the inequality $7 < x$. Check True if the number is in the solution set of the inequality. Check False if it is not.

Value of x	True	False
-2		
12		
0		
8		

5. Tommy can spend, at most, $20.00 at the video arcade.

Part A: Write an inequality to represent how much money, m, Tommy can spend at the arcade.

Part B: Graph the inequality on a number line.

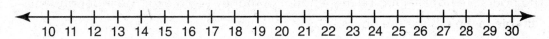

6. Choose the inequality that represents −4 < n. Circle the letter that identifies the correct number line.

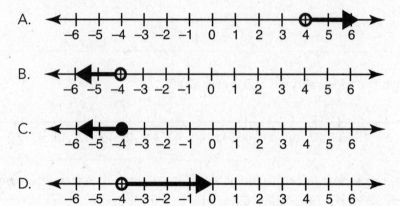

A.

B.

C.

D.

(Answers are on pages 239–240.)

Independent and Dependent Variables

As part of the Common Core Standards, students should be able to identify the independent and dependent variables from tables or graphs. In this section, you will be given strategies that will help you identify each variable. The **dependent variable** is the number or value that is affected by the independent variable. The **independent variable** is the number that stands alone and is not affected by other variables in the problem. Here's an example to show what this means.

Hours	1	5	10	15	20
Dollars Earned	$9.50	$47.50	$95.00	$142.50	$190.00

In the above table, how many dollars you make depends on how many hours you work. The amount of money you make, in this example, is the dependent variable. The hours are not affected by the amount of money you make. The independent variable in the table is the hours.

 **SBAC HINT**

You will also be asked to write an algebraic equation from a table or graph.

You can use the information in the table above to write an equation. Let *d* equal the dollars earned, and let *h* equal the hours:

$$d = 9.5h$$

To prove that you have written the correct equation, go back to the table and substitute one of the *h*-values. In this case, if you substitute 5 for *h*, you will multiply 9.5(5) and get $47.50. This illustrates that your equation is written correctly.

Practice Exercises—Independent and Dependent Variables

Common Core Standard 6.EE.C.9 Use variables to represent two quantities in a real-world problem that change in relationship to one another; write an equation to express one quantity, thought of as the dependent variable, in terms of the other quantity, thought of as the independent variable. Analyze the relationship between the dependent and independent variables using graphs and tables, and relate these to the equation. For example, in a problem involving motion at constant speed, list and graph ordered pairs of distances and times, and write the equation $d = 65t$ to represent the relationship between distance and time.

1. Use the following table to identify the independent variable, the dependent variable, and the equation that identifies the relationship between the churros sold, *c*, to the dollars, *d*, earned.

Churros Sold	50	100	150	200
$ Earned	$25	$50	$75	$100

Part A: Independent variable

```

```

Part B: Dependent variable

```

```

Part C: Equation

```

```

(Answers are on page 241.)

PRACTICE REVIEW TEST:
Expressions and Equations

1. Write the following exponential powers in the appropriate boxes.

$$4^2 \qquad 5^3 \qquad 2.2^4 \qquad 3^5 \qquad \left(\frac{1}{6}\right)^4 \qquad 7^2$$

Less than 20	Between 20 and 100	Greater than 100

2. Use the expression $3x + 7y - 18$ to do the following.

   Part A: Identify the constant.

   Part B: Identify both coefficients.

   Part C: Identify the number of terms in the expression.

3. Kendrell downloaded 12 apps the first day he owned his phone and 9 apps every day thereafter. Write an expression that shows the number of apps he downloaded after x days.

4. Evaluate the following expression when $x = 7$ and $y = 4$.

   $3^4 - (6x + y)$

5. Joshua says that $3(4x + 12)$ is equivalent to $12x + 12$. He states that if you distribute the 3 times the $4x$, that equals $12x$. Do you agree with Joshua's thinking? Why or why not?

6. Select all the expressions that are equivalent to $12x + 10$. Check all that apply.

   A. $(6x + 2)2$ _____

   B. $6x + 7 + 3 + 2(3x)$ _____

   C. $4(3x + 2.5)$ _____

   D. $x + x + 13 + 5x + 7x - 3 - 4x$ _____

   E. $2(6x + 5)$ _____

7. Solve: $7^2 - (54 \div 9) + 23$

8. Anthony has a jar that is filled with 438 candies. On a sleepover last week, his friends ate 227 of the candies. Write an equation that shows how many candies, c, are left. Solve the equation.

   Equation: _____

   Solution: _____

9. Put a check next to all of the following equations that have 9 as a solution.

   A. $23 - n = 14$ _____

   B. $11n = 99$ _____

   C. $17 = 8 + n$ _____

   D. $n \div 4 = 36$ _____

10. Complete the table for the inequality $10 > x$. Check True if the number is in the solution set of the inequality. Check False if it is not.

Value of x	True	False
17		
-5		
9		
11		

11. Joanna earns less than $54 per shift from her local fast food job. Let d represent the amount of money Joanna earns per shift.

   Part A: Write an inequality for how much Joanna earns per shift.

   Part B: Graph the inequality on the following number line.

   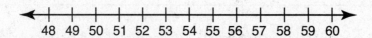

   48 49 50 51 52 53 54 55 56 57 58 59 60

12. Use the following table to identify the independent variable, the dependent variable, and the equation relating the cost to the number of packs of gum purchased.

Packs of Gum (g)	1	2	3	4	5
Cost (c)	$1.25	$2.50	$3.75	$5.00	$6.25

Part A: Independent variable

Part B: Dependent variable

Part C: Write an equation relating the cost, c, to the number of packs of gum purchased, g.

13. A plumber charges $85 for each service call that is less than or equal to an hour. Any hours thereafter are charged at the rate of $50 an hour.

Part A: Write the equation that identifies the cost, c, after t hours.

Part B: How much money would the plumber be paid if he worked for $3\frac{1}{2}$ hours?

14. Find the value of $3m - 5$ if $m = 9$.

15. Brooke's cell phone plan charges a monthly fee of $24.95 and $0.20 per text message, t, sent. What is the monthly cost of Brooke's cell phone plan if she sends 70 texts messages in a month?

16. Select the expression below that has the same value as 5^4.

A. _____ $4 \cdot 4 \cdot 4 \cdot 4 \cdot 4$

B. _____ $5 \cdot 4$

C. _____ $5 \cdot 5 \cdot 5 \cdot 5$

D. _____ 54

17. Rewrite the following expression as the sum of two terms: $5(8n + 4j)$.

18. Solve the following for n.
$$\frac{4}{5}n = \frac{7}{10}$$

19. The local jewelry store charges $10 for all necklaces and $15 for silver earrings. Write an expression that identifies the cost of buying n necklaces and s silver earrings.

(Answers are on pages 241–244.)

Geometry

In this chapter, you will be learning and answering questions about area, surface area, and volume. You will be asked to find the area of triangles and of different types of quadrilaterals. You will discover the fact that the area of some polygons can be found by decomposing them into triangles and rectangles. You will also have to use what you know about area to find the surface area of different three-dimensional prisms and nets. You will revisit the coordinate plane by creating polygons. Finally, you will be asked to find the volume of three-dimensional figures.

Area of Polygons: Quadrilaterals and Triangles

On the Smarter Balanced Assessment, you will be asked to find the area of right triangles, other triangles, and special quadrilaterals. The dimensions of the sides of the polygons can be whole numbers, fractions, or decimals. Solutions for these problems can include these three types of numbers. Picture two right triangles. It is easy to see that they can be combined to create different quadrilaterals, such as squares, rectangles, or parallelograms. To understand how to find the area of a triangle, first look at finding the area of certain quadrilaterals.

 HELPFUL TIP

In the primary grades, the area of a rectangle is usually found by multiplying the length by the width. In middle school, those two factors are recognized as the base and the height. The formula $A = b \times h$ is used to find the area of a rectangle, square, or parallelogram, where A equals the area, b equals the base, and h equals the height.

Example: What is the area of the following quadrilateral?

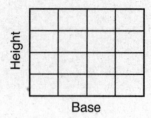

Base

Solution: 16 square units. Either count the squares or use the formula base × height to find the area.

Example: What is the area of the following quadrilateral?

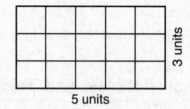

3 units

5 units

Solution: 15 units². Either count the squares or use the formula base × height to find the area.

Example: What is the area of the following quadrilateral?

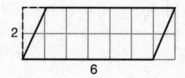

2

6

Solution: 12 square units. Use the formula base × height to find the area.

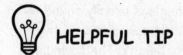 **HELPFUL TIP**

The height of any polygon is measured from the base straight up to the top. It is not the length of a diagonal or slanted line.

The area of a triangle can be found by **decomposing** it. When you decompose a shape, you divide it into smaller shapes. In the following three shapes, a diagonal can be drawn to create two identical triangles.

Shape A:

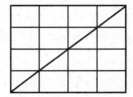

In shape A, the total area is 16 square units. The area of each of the two identical triangles is 8 square units.

Shape B:

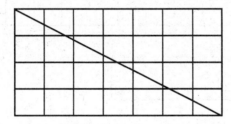

In shape B, the total area is 28 square units. The area of each of the two identical triangles is 14 square units.

Shape C:

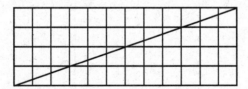

In shape C, the total area is 48 square units. The area of each of the two identical triangles is 24 square units.

Notice that the area of shape A equals the sum of the areas of the two identical triangles into which shape A was divided. The same applies to shape B and to shape C. Remember that the area of a quadrilateral is $A = b \times h$. Since each of the two triangles in the previous three shapes represents half of its quadrilateral, the formula $A = \frac{1}{2}(b \times h)$ can be used to find the area of any triangle.

Practice Exercises—Area of Polygons: Quadrilaterals and Triangles

Common Core Standard 6.G.A.1 Find the area of right triangles, other triangles, special quadrilaterals, and polygons by composing into rectangles or decomposing into triangles and other shapes; apply these techniques in the context of solving real-world and mathematical problems.

1. What is the area of the following quadrilateral?

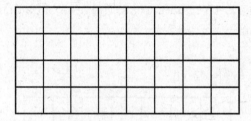

Area = _____

2. What is the area of the following quadrilateral?

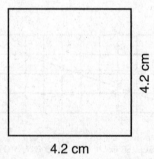

4.2 cm

4.2 cm

Area = _____

3. What is the area of the following quadrilateral?

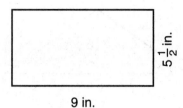

9 in.

Area = _____

4. What is the area of the following quadrilateral?

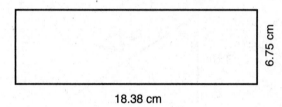

18.38 cm

Area = _____

5. What is the area of the following triangle?

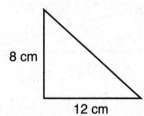

8 cm

12 cm

Area = _____

6. What is the area of the following triangle?

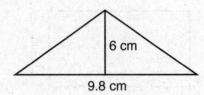

Area = _____

7. What is the area of the following triangle?

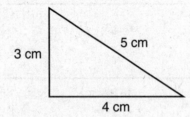

Area = _____

8. What is the area of the following triangle?

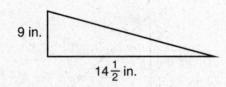

Area = _____

(Answers are on pages 244–245.)

Area of Irregular Polygons

You will have to find the area of various triangles, special quadrilaterals, and other polygons when solving mathematical and real-world problems. The area of these polygons can be found by decomposing the figure into triangles and quadrilaterals with whole-number, decimal, or fraction measures.

Example: The sixth graders at Conway Middle School created an irregularly shaped garden. Find the area of the garden.

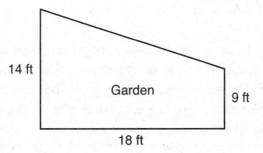

One way to approach this problem is by decomposing the shape into a rectangle and a triangle.

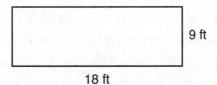

The area for the rectangle is 18 × 9 = 162 square feet.

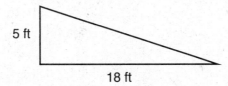

The area for the triangle is calculated by multiplying $\frac{1}{2}(b \times h)$.

$$\frac{1}{2} \times 18 \times 5 = 45 \text{ square feet}$$

The total area for the irregularly shaped garden is 162 + 45 = 207 square feet.

The above garden is in the form of a **trapezoid**. A trapezoid is a quadrilateral with exactly one pair of parallel sides. The formula for finding the area of a trapezoid is $\frac{1}{2}(b_1 + b_2) \times h$. Use this formula to find the area of the irregularly shaped garden.

The length of one of the bases, b_1, is 14 feet. The length of the other base, b_2, is 9 feet. The height, h, is 18 feet.

$$\frac{1}{2}(14 + 9) \times 18$$

$$\frac{1}{2} \times 23 \times 18$$

$$11.5 \times 18 = 207 \text{ square feet}$$

 **HELPFUL TIP**

The b_1 and the b_2 are used to identify the top base and the bottom base of the trapezoid. These are the two sides of the trapezoid that are parallel to each other. The top and bottom bases are not diagonal line segments. You can let either one of the parallel sides be b_1. Then the other parallel side is b_2.

Practice Exercises—Area of Irregular Polygons

Common Core Standard 6.G.A.1 Find the area of right triangles, other triangles, special quadrilaterals, and polygons by composing into rectangles or decomposing into triangles and other shapes; apply these techniques in the context of real-world and mathematical problems.

1. The following quadrilateral is called a kite. Find the area of the kite *ABCD* in square centimeters.

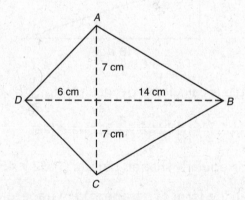

Area = _____

2. What is the area of the following polygon?

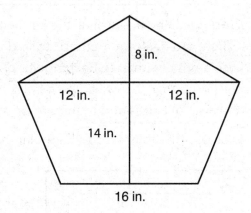

8 in.

12 in.   12 in.

14 in.

16 in.

Area = _____

3. What is the area of the following shape?

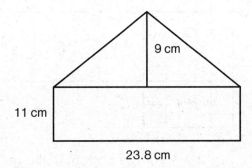

9 cm

11 cm

23.8 cm

Area = _____

(Answers are on page 245.)

Surface Area

Surface area is found by adding all the areas of all the surfaces, or sides, of any three-dimensional figure. There are different methods to find the surface area of a figure. One way is to use a net or a model. Rectangular prisms are the most common three-dimensional figure that you will come across. However, you might also have to find the surface area of cubes and triangular prisms.

Example: Find the surface area of the following rectangular prism.

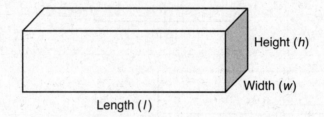

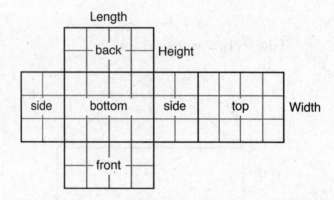

Solution: $2(l \times w) + 2(l \times h) + 2(w \times h)$. The bottom of the rectangular prism can be found by multiplying the length (l) times the width (w). The top of the prism has the same area as the bottom. To find the combined areas of both the top and bottom, either add their combined areas or multiply the area of the top or the bottom by 2 to form $(l \times w) + (l \times w) = 2lw$ or $(l \times w \times 2)$.

To find the area of the front and back, multiply the length (l) × height (h). To find their combined areas, either add the areas together $(l \times h) + (l \times h) = 2lh$ or multiply one of these sides by 2 to form $(l \times h \times 2)$.

To find the areas for the sides, multiply the width (w) × height (h). Again, you will either add their areas together or multiply both areas by 2 to form

$$(w \times h) + (w \times h) = 2wh \text{ or } (w \times h \times 2)$$

To find the total surface area, add the combined areas together:

$$2(l \times w) + 2(l \times h) + 2(w \times h)$$

 **HELPFUL TIP**

Notice that some of the sides of a rectangular prism have the same measures. This will help when computing or adding the areas together. Remember that your answer must be written in square units because you are finding the area of all the sides combined. Be aware that sides can also be called **faces**.

Example: Find the surface area of the following rectangular prism.

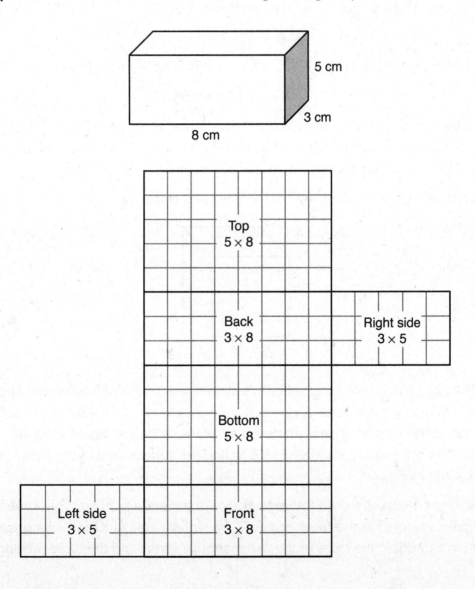

Solution: 158 square centimeters. First identify the sides. The length is 8 cm. The width is 3 cm. The height is 5 cm. The area of the front can be found by multiplying the length of the prism by the height of the prism. Since the front and back are the same, multiply this product by 2: ($l \times h \times 2$).

$$8 \times 5 \times 2 = 80$$

The area of the two sides of the prism can be found by multiplying the width by the height of the prism. Multiply this by 2, because you have two sides ($w \times h \times 2$).

$$3 \times 5 \times 2 = 30$$

The area of the top and the bottom of the prism can be found by multiplying the length by the width of the prism. Remember to multiply this product by 2, because there is a top and a bottom of your prism ($l \times w \times 2$).

$$8 \times 3 \times 2 = 48$$

Once you have found the areas for all the sides, add them together.

$$80 + 30 + 48 = 158$$

A **cube** is another three-dimensional shape. Since all the sides in a cube are the same, the surface area can be found by finding the area of one side and multiplying it by 6. The formula for the surface area of a cube is $SA = 6s^2$.

Example: What is the surface area of the following cube?

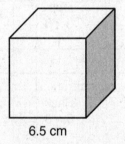

6.5 cm

Solution: 253.5 square centimeters. To find the surface area of a cube, first find the area of one of the sides ($s \times s$): $6.5 \times 6.5 = 42.25$ cm^2. All the sides in a cube have the same area, because each side is a square. Once you have found the area for one of the sides, multiply it by 6 to find the surface area of the cube: $42.25 \times 6 = 253.5$ cm^2.

You might be asked to find the surface area of a triangular prism. This three-dimensional figure has five faces or sides. The surface area of a triangular prism can be found by adding the areas of the two triangular bases and the three rectangular sides. In some cases, the three rectangular sides are congruent or equal in size. In other situations, the rectangular sides are all different in size.

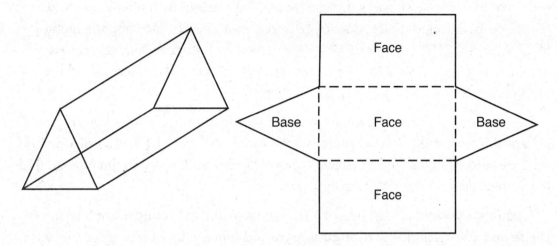

Example: Find the surface area for the following triangular prism. In this specific example, use $\frac{1}{2}(b \times h) \times 2$ to represent the area of both triangular bases. The second formula $3(l \times w)$ represents the area of the three rectangular sides. Combine both solutions to illustrate the total surface area of the triangular prism.

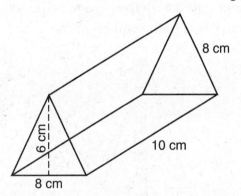

Solution: 288 cm². To find the surface area for this triangular prism, combine the areas for all the sides. Two of the sides, or faces, are triangles. Three of the sides, or faces, are rectangles. The triangles in the above prism have bases of 8 centimeters and heights of 6 centimeters. To find the area of each triangle, use the formula $A = \frac{1}{2}(b \times h)$.

$$\frac{1}{2} \times 6 \times 8$$

$$\frac{1}{2}(48) = 24 \text{ square inches}$$

Since there are two triangular bases, multiply the area of one base by 2: $24 \times 2 = 48$ cm^2. The other three sides are rectangles, each with lengths of 10 and widths of 8. The area for each of these faces can be found by multiplying $l \times w$. Once you have found the product of 10 and 8, multiply it by 3 to find the area of all of the sides: $3(10 \times 8) = 3(80) = 240$ square centimeters. Finally, add the two products together: $48 + 240 = 288$. This represents the total surface area of the triangular prism.

The last type of prism that you might have to find the surface area for is a **pyramid.** A pyramid is a three-dimensional figure where the base is a polygon and the sides are triangles. There are two types of pyramids that you might have to find the surface area on the SBAC Assessment.

A **square pyramid** is made up of a square base and four **congruent** (the same shape and size) triangles. A **triangular pyramid** is made up of four sides that are all triangles. All the faces in a triangular pyramid can be equal, or the base can differ from the other three faces.

Example: Find the surface area of the figure below. Use the formula $A = \frac{1}{2}(b \times h) \times 4 + s^2$. The first part of the equation, $\frac{1}{2}(b \times h) \times 4$, represents the surface area of the four triangles in the pyramid. The second part of the equation, s^2, represents the area of the square base.

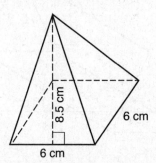

Solution: 138 cm^2. Find the area of the base ($s \times s$ or s^2). Then find the area for the 4 congruent triangles. For this pyramid, the base area can be found by multiplying $6 \times 6 = 36$ cm^2. Use the formula $A = \frac{1}{2}(b \times h)$ to find the area of each triangle. Since all the triangles are the same, multiply the area for one of them by 4.

$$4 \times \frac{1}{2}(6 \times 8.5)$$

$$4 \times 3 \times 8.5 = 102$$

102 cm^2 is the combined surface area of the four triangles. Finally, add the areas together to get the surface area of the square pyramid: $36 + 102 = 138$.

Example: Find the surface area of the figure below.

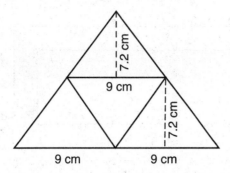

Solution: 129.6 cm². To find the area of an equilateral triangular pyramid, calculate the area of any of the four faces. Since all the sides, or faces, are equivalent, multiply one of the areas by 4. Use the formula $A = \frac{1}{2}(b \times h)$ to find the area of one of the faces.

$$\frac{1}{2} \times 9 \times 72$$

$$4.5 \times 7.2 = 32.4 \text{ cm}^2$$

Finally, multiply $32.4 \times 4 = 129.6$.

Practice Exercises—Surface Area

Common Core Standards 6.G.A.4 Represent three-dimensional figures using nets made up of rectangles and triangles, and use the nets to find the surface area of these figures. Apply these techniques in the context of solving real-world and mathematical problems.

1. Find the surface area of the square pyramid below.

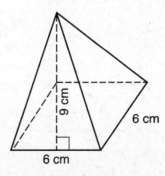

Surface area = _____

2. Find the surface area of the rectangular prism below.

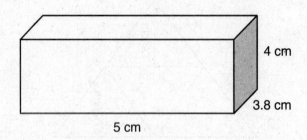

5 cm

Surface area = _____

3. Find the surface area of the cube below.

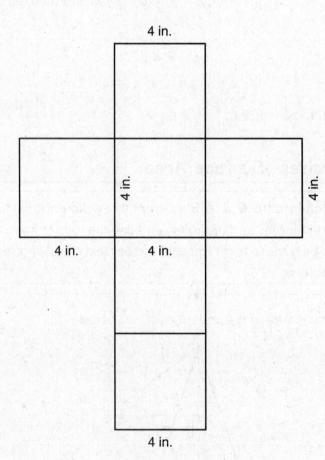

Surface area = _____

4. Find the surface area of the triangular prism below.

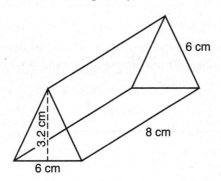

6 cm

3.2 cm

8 cm

6 cm

Surface area = _____

5. A flower company is designing two new packages to carry long-stem roses. Each box is in the shape of a rectangular prism. Complete the table below from information given about box A and box B.

Box A:

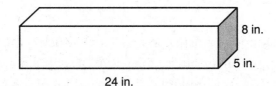

8 in.

5 in.

24 in.

Box B:

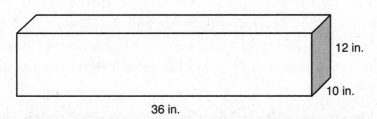

12 in.

10 in.

36 in.

Statement	True	False
The surface area of box B is $1\frac{1}{2}$ times larger than the surface area of box A.		
$2(24 \times 5) + 2(24 \times 8) + 2(5 \times 8)$ can be used to find the surface area of box A.		
The area of the base of box B is three times larger than the area of the base of box A.		

(Answers are on pages 246–247.)

Volume

Now that you understand how to find the area of two-dimensional shapes, that knowledge will be used to help you find the volume of three-dimensional figures. **Volume** measures the number of cubes that can fit inside of a figure or the amount of actual space inside of a figure. Examples of this include how much water fills up a fish tank, how much cereal goes inside of a cereal box, and how much space is inside of a classroom. On the SBAC Assessment, you will be asked to find the volume of rectangular and triangular prisms.

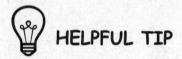 **HELPFUL TIP**

The volume of any figure can be found by pushing the floor (base) of that figure straight up to the ceiling (top of the figure). Once you have found the area of the base, multiply it by the height of the prism. The volume of any prism is always measured in cubic units.

The volume of a rectangular prism can be found by using the formula $V = l \times w \times h$. Multiplying the length by the width gives the area of the base (floor). Once you have found that area, multiply it by the height of the prism. This is another way of taking the floor of your prism and pushing it straight up to the ceiling.

Example: Tina was given a new fish tank for her birthday. She would like to find out the amount of water needed to fill the tank. The measurements of the tank are 32 inches long, 20 inches wide, and 24 inches tall. What is the volume of the fish tank?

Solution: 15,360 in.^{3}. Tina first needs to find out the area of the floor. She can do this by multiplying the length times the width: $32 \times 20 = 640$ square inches. Then she needs to multiply the base area times the height of the fish tank: $640 \times 24 = 15,360$. Remember that the volume of any prism is the measurement of a three-dimensional figure. The unit is always cubed. The amount of water needed to fill the tank is 15,360 cubic inches.

Example: The dimensions of a shoebox are a length of $11\frac{1}{2}$ inches, a width of $6\frac{1}{2}$ inches, and a height of 4 inches. What is the volume of the shoebox?

Solution: 299 in.^{3}. Find the volume by first calculating the area of the base. That area can be found by multiplying $11\frac{1}{2} \times 6\frac{1}{2} = 74\frac{3}{4}$ in.^{2}. Then multiply $74\frac{3}{4} \times 4 = 299$ in.^{3}.

Remember that you are finding how many cubes go inside the figure when you are determining volume. In the previous example, this means that 299 cubes fit inside the shoebox. Each of the six sides of the cube measures 1 inch, as shown in the following figure.

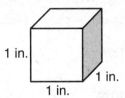

1 in.   1 in.   1 in.

The volume of a triangular prism can be found by using the formula $V = \frac{1}{2}(b \times h) \times l$. Notice that the first part is the formula for finding the area of a triangle. Since the base in a triangular prism is a triangle, first find the surface area of that face. Once you have found the area of the triangular base, multiply that value by the length, or the actual height of the prism (pushing the floor to the ceiling).

Example: What is the volume of the following triangular prism?

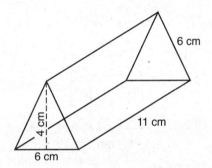

6 cm

4 cm   11 cm

6 cm

Solution: 132 cm³. Find the volume of the triangular prism by taking the area of the base and multiplying it by the height of the figure. The area of the base can be found by finding the area of the triangle. Use the formula $A = \frac{1}{2}(b \times h)$.

$$\frac{1}{2}(6 \times 4) = 3 \times 4 = 12 \text{ cm}^2$$

Then multiply 12 cm by the height of the prism, 11 cm: 12 × 11 = 132. Even though the area of the base is in square units, the solution must be in cubic units because you are finding how much three-dimensional space (volume) is inside of the prism.

Example: Stuart and Bob would like to find the volume of the tent they are going to use on their camping trip. The tent is in the shape of a triangular prism. The triangle measurements include a base of 5 feet and a height of 4 feet. The length of the tent is 10.5 feet. What is the volume of the tent?

Solution: 105 ft³. Find the volume of the triangular prism by taking the area of the base and multiplying it by the height or length of the tent. The base of the prism is triangular: $A = \frac{1}{2}(b \times h) = \frac{1}{2}(5 \times 4) = 10$. Use the length to find the volume because the tent sits on the ground. The two triangular bases are not considered the top and the bottom as in most other cases. Finally, multiply the base area by the length: $10 \times 10.5 = 105$.

Practice Exercises—Volume

Common Core Standard 6.G.A.2 Find the volume of a right rectangular prism with fractional edge lengths by packing it with unit cubes of the appropriate unit fraction edge lengths, and show that the volume is the same as would be found by multiplying the edge lengths of the prism. Apply the formulas $V = l \times w \times h$ and $V = b \times h$ to find the volumes of right rectangular prisms with fractional edge lengths in the context of solving real-world and mathematical problems.

1. What is the volume of the following cube?

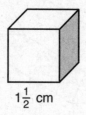

$1\frac{1}{2}$ cm

Volume = _____

2. What is the volume of the following rectangular prism?

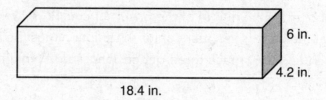

6 in.

4.2 in.

18.4 in.

Volume = _____

3. What is the volume of the following triangular prism?

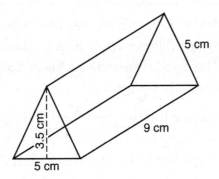

Volume = _____

4. A warehouse storage room is in the shape of a rectangular prism and has 1,152 ft³ of space inside. The length of the room is 18 feet, and the width is 8 feet.

Part A: What is the height of the room?

Part B: All of the boxes that will be stored in the room have the same measurements: 3 feet long, 2 feet wide, and 2 feet high. How many boxes will fit inside of the storage room?

5. What is the volume of the figure below?

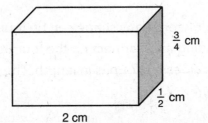

(Answers are on pages 247–248.)

Polygons on the Coordinate Plane

In Chapter 1, you were asked to plot and identify points on the coordinate plane. You will now be asked to create different polygons on the coordinate plane by connecting those points. Once you have created these polygons, you will be asked to find the perimeter or area of those figures.

The **perimeter** of any figure is the length around that figure. You can find the perimeter by adding all the sides together. Remember that you can find the distance from one point to another by counting the units, or you can use an absolute value expression.

Example: Plot the following points on the coordinate plane below. Then identify the perimeter of *ABCD*.

Point *A* (3, 2)

Point *B* (3, –5)

Point *C* (–4, –5)

Point *D* (–4, 2)

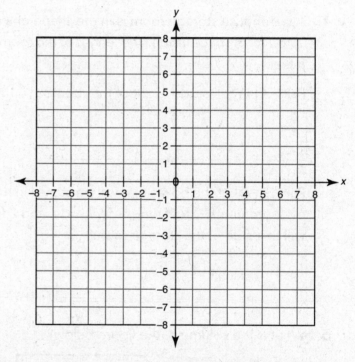

Solution: 28 units. The perimeter of any shape can be found by adding all the side lengths together. After plotting and connecting the four points, the shape that is formed is a square. All four sides are 7 units in length. The perimeter can be found with either 7 + 7 + 7 + 7 or 4 × 7.

Practice Exercises—Polygons on the Coordinate Plane

Common Core Standard 6.G.A.3 Draw polygons in the coordinate plane given coordinates for the vertices; use coordinates to find the length of a side joining points with the same first coordinate or the same second coordinate. Apply techniques in the context of solving real-world and mathematical problems.

1. Plot the following points on the coordinate plane below. (Note: When you take the exam on computer, you will be told to use the Add Point and Connect Line tools.)

   Point A (2, 6)   Point C (11, 1)

   Point B (5, 6)   Point D (2, 1)

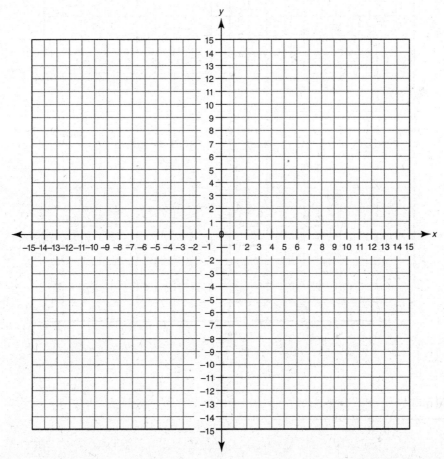

Find the area of the trapezoid using the formula $A = \frac{1}{2}(b_1 + b_2) \times h$.

Area = _____

2. Plot the following points on the coordinate plane below. Find the area of the rectangle.

Point *A* (2, 4)

Point *B* (7, 4)

Point *C* (7, −5)

Point *D* (2, −5)

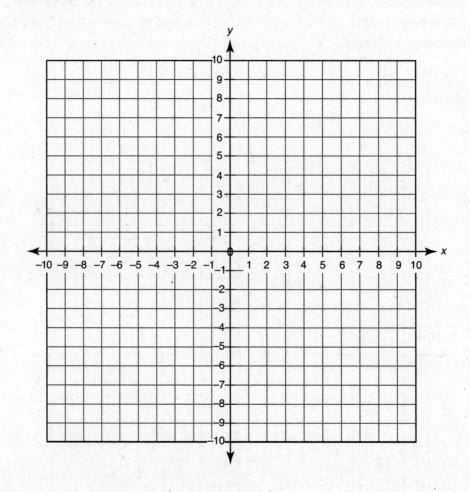

Area = _____

3. Plot the following points on the coordinate plane below. (Note: When you take the exam on computer, you will be told to use the Add Point and Connect Line tools.)

Point *A* (2, 4)

Point *B* (2, 1)

Point *C* (10, 1)

Find the area of the triangle.

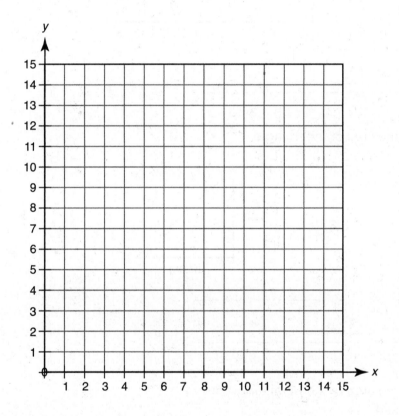

Area = _____

(Answers are on pages 248–250.)

PRACTICE REVIEW TEST:
Geometry

1. Find the area of the figure.

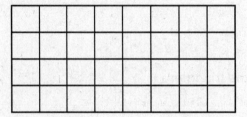

Area = _____

2. Find the area of the triangle.

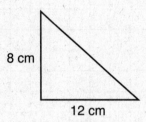

8 cm

12 cm

Area = _____

3. Find the area of the parallelogram.

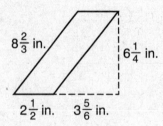

$8\frac{2}{3}$ in. $6\frac{1}{4}$ in.

$2\frac{1}{2}$ in. $3\frac{5}{6}$ in.

Area = _____

4. A rectangular room has an area of 592 square centimeters and a base of 18.5 centimeters.

   Part A: Write an equation that relates the area to the base and height, h.

   Part B: Solve the equation to find the height, h.

5. Use the formula $\frac{1}{2}(b_1 + b_2) \times h$ to find the area of the trapezoid.

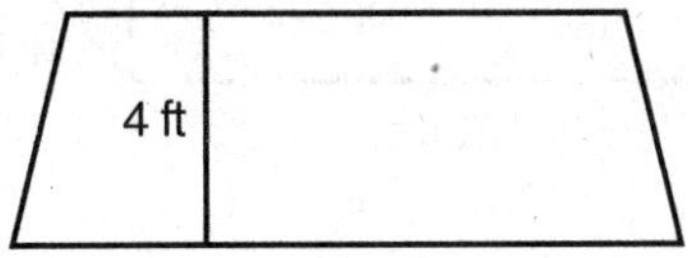

Area = _____

6. Find the area of the rectangle.

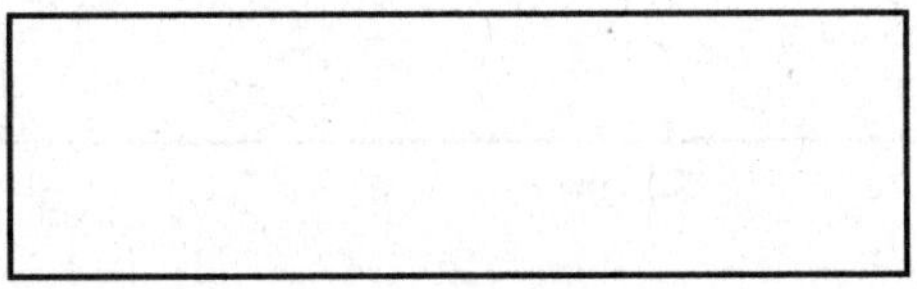

Area = _____

7. Find the area of the parallelogram.

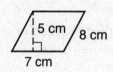

5 cm 8 cm

7 cm

Area = _____

8. The volume of the rectangular prism below is 351 in.^{3} What is the width?

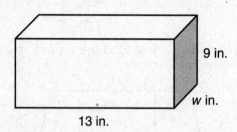

9 in.

w in.

13 in.

Width = _____

9. Find the surface area of the figure.

11 cm

8.5 cm

34 cm

Surface area = _____

10. Find the area of the triangle.

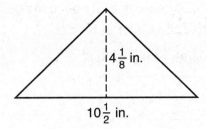

$4\frac{1}{8}$ in.

$10\frac{1}{2}$ in.

Area = _____

11. Find the surface area of the pyramid below.

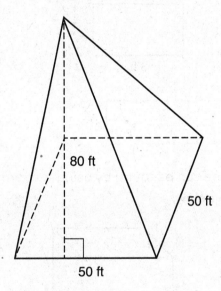

80 ft

50 ft

50 ft

Surface area = _____

12. A file cabinet has a base area of 424.6 in.² What is the volume of the cabinet if its height is 54 inches?

Volume = _____

13. The Pacheco family is moving to a new city. They have rented a trailer for the move. The trailer has 420 cubic feet of space inside. The height of the trailer is 7 feet, and the length of the trailer is 10 feet.

Part A: What is the width of the trailer?

Width = _____

Part B: The Pacheco family used the same size box, as pictured below, to pack all their belongings. If the family stacks the boxes any way they like, what is the maximum number of boxes that will completely fill the trailer?

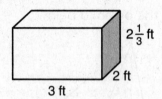

$2\frac{1}{3}$ ft

2 ft

3 ft

Boxes = _____

14. The volume of a cube can be found by using the formula $V = s^3$. Find the volume of the cube below.

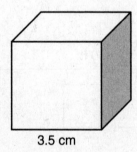

3.5 cm

Volume = _____

15. Use the grid to plot the following points:

Point A (4, 3)

Point B (4, 9)

Point C (10, 9)

Point D (14, 3)

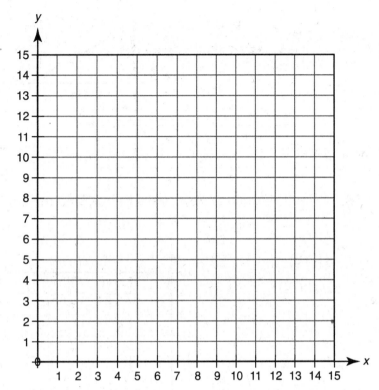

Connect the points to form quadrilateral *ABCD*. Use the formula

$A = \frac{1}{2}(b_1 + b_2) \times h$ to find the area of the constructed figure.

Area = _____

16. Tia and Andy have created two different-sized candy boxes. They are trying to figure out which box holds more candy. Both of their candy boxes are in the shape of a rectangular prism. Tia's candy box has a length of 4 inches, a width of $1\frac{1}{2}$ inches, and a height of 6 inches. Andy's candy box has a length of 5 inches, a width of 2 inches, and a height of 4 inches. Whose box holds more candy, Tia's or Andy's? Why?

17. Find the area of the triangle.

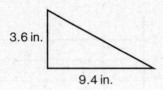

3.6 in.

9.4 in.

Area = _____

18. Graph the three ordered pairs below. Find the area of triangle *HIJ*.

H (2, 4)

I (7, 8)

J (11, 4)

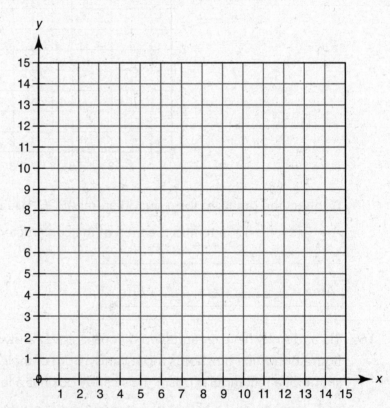

Area = _____

(Answers are on pages 250–254.)

Statistics

Statistics is the collection and study of **data**, which are factual information that can be used in calculations or reasoning. Statistics is used in many ways. Compiling the ages of every student in your school, figuring out which months of the year have the most rain, or even surveying classmates to find out their favorite flavors of ice cream are just some of the ways you can find data in our society. Analyzing data helps us make predictions about future events. Data can help volleyball coaches identify the most productive players on their team. Data help a pizza company figure out how much pepperoni it needs to buy. Data can help you figure out what kind of clothing to wear on a sunny day. Data are everywhere. Sixth-grade students should know how to identify if a question is statistical or not, find different **measures of central tendency** (the way data cluster around the center value), and summarize or display data using a variety of models.

Statistical Questions

When working with data, you must be able to identify if a question is statistical or not. Statistical questions include a variety of answers. When determining if a question is statistical, identify the number of answers. If there is one factual answer or one numerical solution, the question is *not* statistical.

For example, if you ask Matthew how many movies he saw over the summer, that would *not* be a statistical question. He watched a specific number of movies. Whether the number was 3, 5, or 12, the number of movies Matthew saw is definitive. If you want to know how many movies each student in a class of thirty saw over the summer, you will get various answers. That type of question is therefore a statistical question.

There are two different types of statistical questions: numerical and categorical.

One type of statistical question involves a numerical answer. Finding the age of students at Lincoln Middle School is a statistical question that includes a numerical answer. A categorical question is one where the answers are represented in words.

The table below identifies statistical questions for each category.

Numerical Questions	Categorical Questions
Ages of students in middle school	Favorite breakfast cereal
Height of sixth graders	Favorite color
Number of siblings per student	Favorite sport

Practice Exercises—Statistical Questions

Common Core Standard 6.SP.A.1 Recognize a statistical question as one that anticipates variability in the data related to the question and accounts for it in the answers. *For example, "How old am I?" is not a statistical question, but "How old are the students in my school?" is a statistical question because one anticipates variability in students' ages.*

Determine if questions 1–4 are statistical or not. Explain your reasoning.

1. How many minutes are in an hour?

2. What is the height of all the seventh graders at Thompson Middle School?

3. How many football players are on the Packers Team?

4. What is the favorite sport of each of the 1,400 middle school students at Cortez Middle School?

5. Complete the table below. Identify whether or not the question is statistical. Check Yes if it is statistical. Check No if the question is not.

Question	Yes	No
How much time do the students in my school spend watching television each night?		
How tall is Mount Everest?		
How old are people when they start to drink coffee?		
How many students earned an A on the last test?		
How many days are in a month?		

(Answers are on page 254.)

Measures of Central Tendency

When looking at or analyzing a set of numbers, the first thing that you often need to do is put the numbers in order from least to greatest. In this section, you will learn about three measures of central tendency: median, mode, and mean.

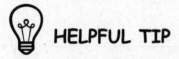 HELPFUL TIP

When writing the numbers from least to greatest, make sure to list all the numbers in your data set. Sometimes numbers occur more than once. If a number occurs three times, make sure it is written three times in your new list. Count both lists to make sure they contain the same amount of numbers in them.

Example: List the numbers 18, 12, 17, 18, 21, 24, 17, 18, 20, and 23 from least to greatest.

Solution: First identify how many numbers are in your data set. There are ten numbers in your set. Then list the numbers from least to greatest.

12, 17, 17, 18, 18, 18, 20, 21, 23, 24

If the total amount of numbers matches, you can then proceed to find different measures.

In statistics, measures of center (or measures of central tendency) help us interpret or draw conclusions about the numbers in our data. Understanding the center gives you critical information about the entire set of numbers. When you analyze data or a group of numbers, you are determining what will happen most of the time. There are three measures of center that you will be asked to find.

The first measure of center is the **median**. The median is the number in the middle when your data values are displayed from least to greatest. To find the median, list the numbers from least to greatest. Then eliminate numbers, one by one, from each side of the list until you get to the middle number. In some cases, there will be two numbers in the middle. The average of those two numbers is the median.

~~16, 17, 18, 18,~~ (20) ~~23, 23, 24, 28~~

In the data set above, the median is 20.

Example: Mrs. Baker's small group of students earned the following grades on their midterm exam: 87%, 91%, 72%, 79%, 81%, 84%, and 95%. What is the median of the grades?

Solution: 84 is the median. First identify how many numbers are in the set of data. The answer is seven. Then list the numbers from least to greatest. Make sure there are seven numbers in your new list.

$$72, 79, 81, 84, 87, 91, 95$$

Start eliminating numbers, one by one, from each side of the group. First you will cross out 72 and 95. Then cross out 79 and 91. Finally, cross out 81 and 87. The number 84 is the median of your data set.

 **HELPFUL TIP**

Remember to first identify the numbers from least to greatest.

If there is an even amount of numbers in your data set, find the average of the two remaining numbers.

Example: Find the median for the following set of numbers.

$$18, 12, 17, 19, 17, 20, 22, 26, 18, 19, 24, 17$$

Solution: 18.5 is the median. First identify how many numbers are in the set of data. There are twelve. Then list the numbers from least to greatest. Make sure there are twelve numbers in your new list. Be careful since some of the numbers repeat.

$$12, 17, 17, 17, 18, 18, 19, 19, 20, 22, 24, 26$$

After crossing out numbers from both sides, the numbers 18 and 19 will be left over. To find the median for those two numbers, calculate their average. The average is calculated by adding the two numbers together and then dividing by 2.

$$18 + 19 = 37$$

$$37 \div 2 = 18.5$$

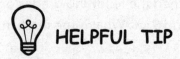 **HELPFUL TIP**

To find the median of any two consecutive numbers, add one-half to the smaller of the two numbers. The median of 9 and 10 is therefore $9\frac{1}{2}$ or 9.5.

The second measure of center is called the **mode**. The mode is the number that occurs most often in your group or set of numbers. To find the mode, it is not necessary to list the numbers from least to greatest. The mode occurs more frequently than any other number.

 **HELPFUL TIP**

In a group of numbers, there can be one specific mode (a number that occurs more than any other number). There can be more than one mode (two numbers that occur more than the rest of the numbers and each one having the same frequency). Sometimes there will be no mode (when all the numbers occur the same amount of time as each other).

Example: Find the mode in the following set of numbers.

23, 38, 29, 40, 17, 23, 30, 23, 28, 36, 39, 21, 25

Solution: The mode is 23. To find the mode, figure out which number occurs most often. The number 23 occurs three times in your data set. All the other numbers, in the set, only occur one time each. The numbers do not have to be in order from least to greatest when finding the mode. It is helpful to list them in order, but not necessary.

17, 21, 23 23 23 25, 28, 29, 30, 36, 38, 39, 40

Example: Find the mode in the following set of numbers.

37, 39, 41, 29, 30, 40, 39, 29, 28, 36

Solution: There are two modes, 29 and 39. The frequency of both 29 and 39 is twice. The other numbers occur only once.

28, ㉙㉙ 30, 36, 37, ㊴㊴ 40, 41

Example: Find the mode in the following set of numbers.

6, 7, 8, 10, 4, 5, 13, 15, 9, 1, 12

Solution: There is no mode. Since all the numbers occur only once, no mode exists for this set of data.

The third measure of center is called the **mean**. The mean is the average of the numbers in your data set. The mean is a statistical data point that is used to find student grades, among other things.

To find the mean, first add all the numbers together in the data set. Then divide that total by how many actual data points, or numbers, are in the group.

Example: Use the following test scores to figure out the mean of Tina's test scores.

86%, 74%, 70%, 90%, 88%, 72%

Solution: 80%. First add all the numbers together.

86 + 74 + 70 + 90 + 88 + 72 = 480

Then divide that number by the number of data points you have.

480 ÷ 6 = 80

Tina's mean, or average, is 80%.

Example: The following shows how many points Ricky scored in each of his eight basketball games this year. Find the mean amount of points Ricky scored in each game.

23, 18, 19, 23, 20, 15, 27, 19

Solution: 20.5. First add all the numbers together.

23 + 18 + 19 + 23 + 20 + 15 + 27 + 19 = 164

Then divide that number by the number of data points you have.

164 ÷ 8 = 20.5

On average, Ricky scored 20.5 points in each of his eight games.

 **SBAC HINT**

On the Smarter Balanced Assessment, you might have to analyze the mean and how a new data point, or number, will affect the average. You might also have to identify a missing value given the mean.

Example: The average number of goals Esperanza scored for her club team was 1.2 goals per game. If Esperanza scores 2 goals in her final soccer game, will her average go up, go down, or stay the same? Explain your reasoning.

Solution: The mean (average) will increase. When adding a data point to an existing set of numbers, first identify if that data point is below, above, or the same as the existing mean. If the mean for a set of data is 90 and you add the number 94, your mean will increase. If instead you add the number 90, the mean will stay the same. If you add a number less than 90, the mean will decrease. In this problem, the data point added to the existing data is larger than the original mean. The existing mean will therefore increase.

Example: For eight pieces of data, the mean is 22. Use the following seven pieces of data to identify the missing data point.

$$20, 27, 19, 20, 21, 24, 20, \_\_\_$$

Solution: 25. To find a missing value, take the mean and multiply it by the number of total numbers in your data set, which is 8.

$$22 \times 8 = 176$$

Then add the initial seven values together.

$$20 + 27 + 19 + 20 + 21 + 24 + 20 = 151$$

Finally, subtract 151 from the product of 22 and 8.

$$176 - 151 = 25$$

Practice Exercises—Measures of Central Tendency

Common Core Standard 6.SP.A.3 Recognize that a measure of center for a numerical data set summarizes all its values with a single number, while a measure of variation describes how its values vary with a single number.

Common Core Standard 6.SP.B.5.A Reporting the number of observations.

1. Find the mean, median, and mode for the following set of numbers.

67, 78, 79, 61, 58, 70, 86, 74, 80, 59, 91, 61

Mean = _____

Median = _____

Mode = _____

2. The following table represents the number of text messages five different sixth graders sent over a month's time.

Name	Text Messages Sent
Rachel	123
Justin	86
Gavin	99
Leslie	80
Gabriella	102

Find the mean number of text messages for the five students.

3. Consider the following set of numbers.

42, 43, 38, 42, 39, 48, 36, 38, 41, 50

52, 50, 50, 39, 32, 37, 53, 40, 31, 38

Find the mode for the data above.

Mode: _____

4. The table shows the number of yards five running backs gained in a football game. The mean number of yards gained, for all five running backs, is 68. How many yards did Merrill gain? Explain how you found your solution.

Player	Number of Yards Gained
Alphonso	124
Germaine	36
Troy	52
Todd	40
Merrill	?

5. Consider the following set of data.

81, 88, 90, 102, 79, 84, 76, 88, 93, 95, 79, 100, 71, 91

Part A: Find the median for the data.

Part B: Find the mode for the data.

Part C: If the number 100 is added to the data, will the mean increase, decrease, or stay the same? Explain your reasoning.

(Answers are on pages 255–256.)

Measures of Variation

Another way to look at data is by analyzing the **spread**, which is the variability of the data. Some examples of spread include how far away the data are from the mean, what are the lowest and highest data points, and even looking at how spread out the information is. **Measures of variation** indicate how spread out or how scattered a set of data is. We look at measures of variation when we want to find how the nature of the data changes within the data set.

One measure of variation is the **range**. This is the difference between the lowest and highest data points. When the range is a large value, the data are very spread out. When the range is a small value, the numbers are very close together or clustered.

💡 HELPFUL TIP

The range is easily found when the numbers are listed from least to greatest. When the numbers are listed in ascending order, the number on the far left is the **minimum** (the smallest value in the data set) and the number on the far right is the **maximum** (the largest value in the data set).

Example: Find the range for the following set of data.

12, 18, 30, 17, 25, 27, 31, 10, 22, 24

Solution: 21. First list the numbers from least to greatest. Remember to identify how many numbers are in your data set. This way you will not forget any numbers when you change the order of the numbers.

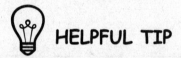 12, 17, 18, 22, 24, 25, 27, 30, 31

The minimum or lowest data point is 10. The maximum or highest data point is 31. Subtract the lowest value from the highest value. The range is 21.

Maximum − Minimum = Range

31 − 10 = 21

A second measure of variation includes the two quartiles. These are called the upper quartile and the lower quartile. The **upper quartile** is the middle of the set of data points above the median. The **lower quartile** is the middle for the set of data points below the median. The word *quartile* comes from the word "quarter." Each quartile represents $\frac{1}{4}$ of the entire set of data.

To find the quartiles, you must first understand how to find the median of the data set. The median splits all the data in half. The quartiles divide those two sections into half again. This creates four sections or parts. Remember that finding the quartiles can be quite simple when there is an odd number of data points. You cross out numbers until you get to the middle. It can be more difficult when there are an even number of data points. When there is an even number of data points, find the mean, or average, of the two numbers in the middle to determine the median.

Example: Find the median, lower quartile, and upper quartile for the following set of numbers.

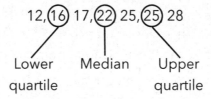

Solution: Median = 22; lower quartile = 16; upper quartile = 25. The median of 22 represents the number in the middle after crossing out data points from each side. Once you have identified the median, find the two quartiles. Since 22 is the middle of the entire set, the data points below 22 are 12, 16, and 17. The middle of that set of numbers is 16. This number is called the lower quartile. The data points above 22 are 25, 25, and 28. The middle of that set of numbers is 25. This number is called the upper quartile.

 **SBAC HINT**

The lower quartile is sometimes represented as Q1, and the upper quartile is sometimes represented as Q3.

Another measure of variation is the **interquartile range**, which is abbreviated as IQR. The interquartile range is the difference between the upper and lower quartiles. The IQR is found by subtracting the lower quartile from the upper quartile.

$$Q3 - Q1 = IQR$$

Example: Find the interquartile range for the following set of data.

41, 43, 56, 29, 37, 50, 48, 36, 42, 51

Solution: 13. First arrange the numbers from least to greatest. Then start crossing out numbers, one by one, from each side of the data set.

29, 36, 37, 41, 42, 43, 48, 50, 51, 56

After crossing out numbers, two numbers will remain in the middle (42 and 43). The average, or mean, of those two numbers is 42.5. This represents the median for the entire data set. Since 42.5 is not in the data set, the numbers below the median include 29, 36, 37, 41, and 42. The middle, or median, of those numbers is 37. This represents the lower quartile (Q1). The numbers above 42.5 include 43, 48, 50, 51, and 56. The middle, or median, of those numbers is 50. This represents the upper quartile (Q3). Finally, subtract the lower quartile from the upper quartile.

$$50 - 37 = IQR = 13$$

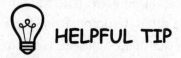 **HELPFUL TIP**

Remember that you must find the median first to identify the upper and lower quartiles.

The last measure of variation that you will be asked to find is the **mean absolute deviation (MAD)**. The mean absolute deviation is the variation, or distance, of each data point from the mean. Finding the MAD requires a few calculations. The steps are listed below.

STEP 1   Find the mean, or average, of the entire data set.

STEP 2   Find the difference between each number in the set and the mean.

STEP 3   Find the average of the differences (absolute deviations).

The MAD identifies how far each number deviates from the mean. This may sound complicated. However, if you understand how to find the mean, you should be able to find the mean absolute deviation.

Example: Find the mean absolute deviation for the following set of numbers.

$$17, 18, 20, 19, 12, 19, 23, 16$$

Solution: 2.25. To find the mean absolute deviation, first find the mean or average. To find the mean, first add all the numbers together.

$$17 + 18 + 20 + 19 + 12 + 19 + 23 + 16 = 144$$

Then divide that sum by the total number of data points.

$$144 \div 8 = 18$$

Now see how far away each data point is from the mean.

$$|18 - 17| = |1| = 1$$

$$|18 - 18| = 0$$

$$|18 - 20| = |-2| = 2$$

$$|18 - 19| = |-1| = 1$$

$$|18 - 12| = |6| = 6$$

$$|18 - 19| = |-1| = 1$$

$$|18 - 23| = |-5| = 5$$

$$|18 - 16| = |2| = 2$$

Now find the mean of these absolute deviations.

$$\frac{1+0+2+1+6+1+5+2}{8} = \frac{18}{8} = 2.25$$

 **HELPFUL TIP**

The difference between the mean and a data point could result in a negative value. Think back to the work you did with absolute values. The word *absolute* means that the direction, or distance, doesn't matter. When finding the deviation from the mean, the difference will always be positive.

Although there are a lot of steps, finding the mean absolute deviation gives you some important information about how spread out your data is.

Practice Exercises—Measures of Variation

Common Core Standard 6.SP.A.3 Recognize that a measure of center for a numerical data set summarizes all its values with a single number, while a measure of variation describes how its values vary with a single number.

1. Consider the following data.

   27, 19, 32, 33, 28, 24, 20, 27, 28, 22, 20

   Part A: Find the upper and lower quartiles.

   Upper quartile: _____

   Lower quartile: _____

   Part B: Find the interquartile range (IQR).

2. Find the mean absolute deviation of the following data.

   8, 10, 7, 6, 13, 5, 14, 1

(Answers are on pages 256–257.)

Box Plots and Other Data Displays

Data displays are visual models of information and come in a variety of forms. You should recognize some of them from previous grades. Others you will see for the first time. Different data displays are used for different reasons. What is important is that each display shows a lot of valuable information about a set of data. Before you create or analyze data, pay close attention to the labels that go with each display. The data displays that will be found on the SBAC Assessment include box plots, dot plots (line plots), and histograms.

A **box plot** is a visual display that separates the data into fourths or quarters. It is a model that is used to represent data or information. Earlier in this chapter, you learned about quartiles and the median. Box plots are one way to display that data.

Five numbers are displayed in a box plot: the **maximum** (the largest value), the **minimum** (the smallest value), the **median**, the **lower quartile**, and the **upper quartile**. This is sometimes called the **five-number summary**. To create a box plot, identify these five numbers from a data set. Then draw your visual display.

Here is how to create a box plot.

1. First draw a number line. Make sure the lowest number is less than the minimum data point and that the highest number is greater than the maximum data point.

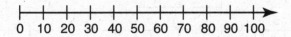

2. After you have listed the data points from least to greatest and have found the five-number summary, plot points above the number line at each of those values.

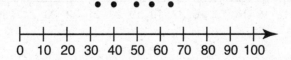

3. Draw a box between the upper and lower quartiles. Split the box, with a vertical line segment, at the median.

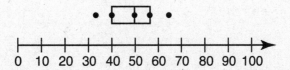

4. Draw two horizontal line segments: one from the upper quartile to the maximum and one from the lower quartile to the minimum.

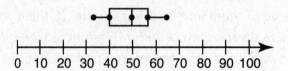

Example: Which box plot displays the data shown in the chart? Circle the correct letter.

15	17	20
15	18	15
26	12	17

A.

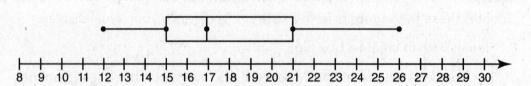

B.

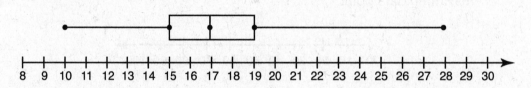

C.

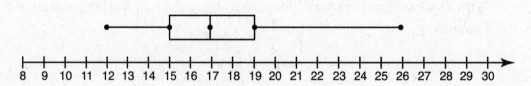

D.

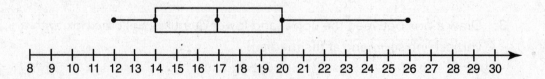

Solution: C. After listing the numbers from least to greatest, the five-number summary includes minimum = 12, maximum = 26, median = 17, lower quartile = 15, and upper quartile = 19. Remember that if there are two numbers for any of the three medians, you must find the average of those two numbers. The upper quartile median is between 18 and 20.

Dot plots, which are also called **line plots**, are another way of displaying data. They show the number of times, or frequency, that something occurs. The data values are marked by an × or a dot for each specific category.

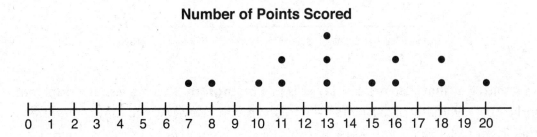

Number of Points Scored

Example: Create a line plot from the following data.

Mr. Sandler asked his sixth-grade students what their favorite sport was. The results are shown below.

Sport	Number of students
Basketball	8
Baseball	10
Soccer	5
Hockey	3
Football	9
Volleyball	4

Solution: See the dot plot below.

Students' Favorite Sports

```
                    X
                    X              X
        X           X              X
        X           X              X
        X           X              X
        X           X       X      X
        X           X  X    X      X      X
        X           X  X    X  X   X      X
        X           X  X    X  X   X      X
        X           X  X    X  X   X      X
     ───┴───────────┴──┴────┴──┴───┴──────┴───
     Basketball  Baseball  Soccer  Hockey  Football  Volleyball
```

A third way that data are displayed is in a **histogram**. This is a visual model that indicates how many data points fall into any given category. You may remember that in previous years, you were asked to create or analyze bar graphs. Each bar represented a specific event. In a histogram, each bar represents an **interval**, which is a set of numbers divided into sections.

 **HELPFUL TIP**

Intervals in a histogram represent all the numbers between two distinct points. For example, intervals could include 1–10, 11–20, and 21–30. Make sure that the numbers don't overlap. Also, there will *not* be any gaps between intervals. The intervals 0–20, 40–60, and 100–120 are *not* acceptable intervals in a histogram.

Example: Create a histogram of the following data points. They show the heights (in inches) of sixth graders in Mr. Wu's third-period class.

54	52	47	49	61
58	64	48	56	53
65	48	57	59	67
70	63	57	59	60

First identify your categories. You want to find out how many students are between 40–49 inches, between 50–59 inches, between 60–69 inches, and between 70–79 inches tall. Then organize your data in a **frequency table**. This is a table that lists how often something occurs in a data set.

Height (inches)	Frequency
40–49	4
50–59	9
60–69	6
70–79	1

Now let's look at a histogram that displays information from the frequency table. A histogram is a visual that illustrates bars of different heights. The bars represent a range of numbers called intervals. The frequency, or number of observations, will be displayed on your vertical axis. The horizontal axis includes the intervals of the event.

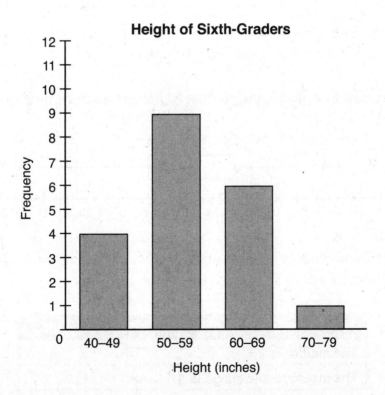

SBAC HINT

You must know how to label a histogram. The vertical axis shows the frequency, and the horizontal axis shows the interval. You may also be asked to analyze a histogram and answer questions about it.

Example: Based on the histogram you created in the previous example, which category had the fewest students? Which category had the most students? How many students were there altogether?

Solution: The fewest number of students were 70–79 inches tall. The largest number of students were 50–59 inches tall. There were 20 students in all. Adding the right column in a frequency table will give you the total number of data points.

Practice Exercises—Box Plots and Other Data Displays

Common Core Standard 6.SP.B.4 Display numerical data in plots on a number line, including dot plots, histograms, and box plots.

1. Alex made a box plot for the number of points he scored throughout the season.

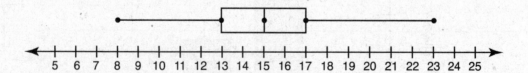

Determine whether or not each statement about data shown in the box plot is true. Select True or False for each statement.

Statement	True	False
The median is 23.		
The interquartile range is 4.		
The minimum is 8.		

2. Use the histogram to answer the questions below.

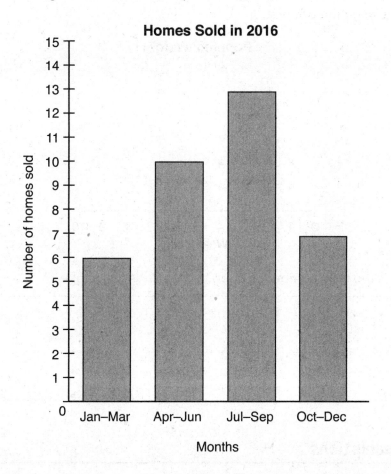

Homes Sold in 2016

Part A: How many homes were sold between April and September?

Part B: Which three-month period had the most home sales?

Part C: How many homes were sold in all?

3. Rhonda is breeding puppies. She weighs each one as it is born. The results are shown in the dot plot.

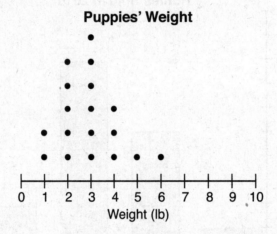

Puppies' Weight

Weight (lb)

What is the total number of puppies that Rhonda weighed?

(Answers are on pages 257–258.)

Data Descriptions

Now that you have looked at measures of central tendency, measures of variation, and different visual models, it is time to describe the data. This is the last step in sixth-grade math to understanding statistics. You will be asked questions about the center, variability, and the shape of the data. Since you have already learned about the first two, let's look at how data are shaped when graphed. When data points are evenly distributed, near the middle, they are said to be **symmetric** in shape. When data points are **skewed right**, most of the data values are concentrated on the left. When data points are **skewed left**, most of the data values are concentrated on the right.

Example: In the pictures below, identify the symmetric data, the data skewed left, and the data skewed right. Write the appropriate word in the box beneath each picture. (Note that on the actual test, you will click and drag the words to match each picture.)

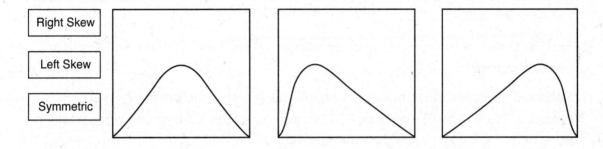

Solution:

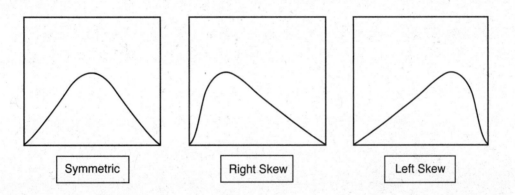

The symmetric data are evenly grouped near the middle of the first graph. The data skewed left are grouped on the right as shown in the third graph. The data skewed right are concentrated on the left as shown in the second graph.

The last data descriptor is an **outlier**. This is a data point that is far away from most of the data values. It is still used when calculating center and spread, but it is sometimes eliminated from the data when calculating the mean.

Example: Consider the following data points.

$$18, 23, 24, 19, 54, 21, 20, 21$$

Part A: Which number is an outlier?

Solution: 54. The number 54 is the outlier because it is very far from the other data points in the set.

Part B: Does the mean increase or decrease if 54 is taken out of the set? Explain your reasoning.

Solution: Decrease. Any time a data point is taken out of the set, it affects the measure. The mean will decrease if 54 is taken out of the set because you are taking out a number that is greater than the mean.

Practice Exercises—Data Descriptions

Common Core Standard 6.SP.B.5.C Giving quantitative measures of center (median and/or mean) and variability (interquartile range and/or mean absolute deviation), as well as describing any overall pattern and any striking deviations from the overall pattern with reference to the context in which the data were gathered.

Common Core Standard 6.SP.B.5.D Relation the choice of measures of center and variability to the shape of the data distribution and the context in which the data were gathered.

Sandra surveyed her friends to see how much time, in hours, they spent reading each week. The results are shown in this line plot.

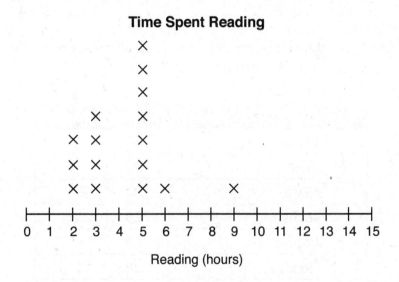

Determine whether each statement about the spread of the data is true. Select True or False for each statement.

Statement	True	False
The data are skewed to the left.		
The data are symmetrical.		
Sandra surveyed sixteen friends.		

(Answers are on page 258.)

PRACTICE REVIEW TEST:
Statistics

1. Isabel and Justin are both unsure whether or not the following question is statistical: How much time do the students at Westchester High spend on homework each night? Isabel reasons that the question is statistical because she feels that there will be more than one answer. Justin thinks that it is not statistical because he doesn't know how much time each student spends on homework. Who is correct? Explain your reasoning.

2. The table shows the number of shoes a group of friends owns. Find the median number of shoes owned.

Name	Number of Shoes Owned
Emilio	16
Kim	21
Sara	37
Rachel	29
Virginia	24
Raul	28

3. Mr. Lopez played golf 10 times last year. Use the table below to answer the following statistical questions.

Round of Golf	1	2	3	4	5	6	7	8	9	10
Score	75	85	88	89	83	77	80	81	83	79

Part A: Find the mean score for Mr. Lopez's rounds of golf.

Part B: Find the mean absolute deviation of the scores.

4. Identify the outlier in the following set of data. Explain your reasoning.

29, 27, 31, 20, 36, 31, 29, 24, 59, 28, 30, 31, 29

5. The following list identifies fifteen student test scores for a midterm exam.

87, 90, 68, 91, 78, 79, 82, 74, 66, 90, 93, 84, 90, 85, 73

Part A: What is the mean?

Part B: What is the median?

Part C: What is the range?

Part D: Louie thinks that the mode is 93 because it is the highest test score. Do you agree with Louie's thinking? Why or why not?

6. Which measure of center (mean, median, or mode) would best describe the following sets of data? Explain your reasoning.

Part A: Ticket prices for a concert:

$48, $30, $40, $35, $45, $50, $42, $38

Part B: Housing prices (in thousands of dollars):

280, 260, 290, 475, 395, 400, 320, 925

Part C: Number of points scored:

17, 15, 16, 20, 16, 16, 19, 16

7. The table below illustrates the number of hours eleven employees worked over a 7-day period.

Employee	Hours Worked
Matthew	36
Jade	28
Nathan	40
Charlene	32
Anthony	35
Keisha	37
Savannah	31
Amanda	28
Simone	34
Ashlee	40
Arthur	27

Which box plot displays the data shown in the chart? Circle the correct letter.

A.

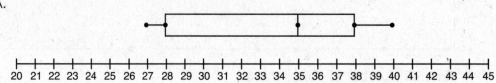

B.

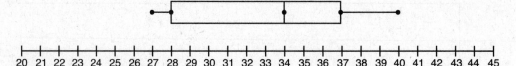

C.

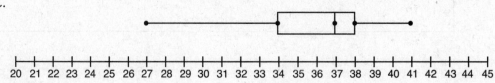

D.

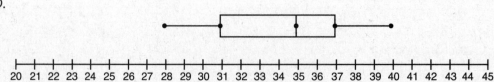

8. Students at the Anton Valley Middle School were asked to sell boxes of candy to help raise money. The line plot illustrates the number of boxes of candy that the sixth-grade class sold. Use the line plot to find the median, mode, and range.

Boxes of Candy Sold

```
                    X
                    X
        X           X     X           X
        X           X  X  X  X  X              X
        X  X        X  X  X  X  X        X  X  X
        +--+--+--+--+--+--+--+--+--+--+--+--+--+--+
        0  1  2  3  4  5  6  7  8  9  10 11 12 13 14
                        Boxes of candy
```

Median = _____

Mode = _____

Range = _____

9. Are the data in the illustration below skewed right, skewed left, or symmetrical? Explain your reasoning.

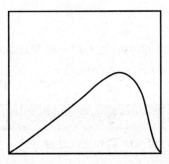

10. Trina made a box plot for the number of points she scored in her team's basketball games. Her box plot is shown below.

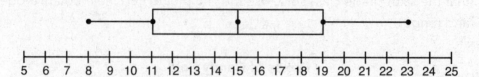

Determine whether each statement about the box plot of the data is true. Select True or False for each statement.

Statement	True	False
The median is 15.		
The upper quartile is 17.		
The interquartile range is 8.		
The range is 19.		

11. Paula surveyed her friends to see how many brothers and sisters they had in their family. The results are in the dot plot shown below.

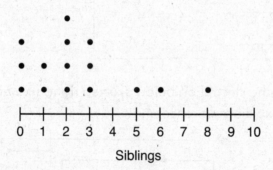

Siblings

Determine whether each statement about the dot plot of the data is true. Select True or False for each statement.

Statement	True	False
The total number of friends surveyed is fifteen.		
The illustration is skewed to the left.		
The dot plot shows a cluster of data from 0–3.		
The data are symmetrical.		

12. Consider the following data.

$$23, 27, 19, 25, 18, 30, 19, 24$$

The number 15 is added to the data set. Determine whether each statement is true or false once this extra number is added. Select True or False for each statement.

Statement	True	False
Adding the extra number will increase the mean.		
Adding the extra number will increase the range.		
Adding the extra number will change the median.		

13. Consider this data set.

9	12	7	13
10	9	14	8
8	12	10	9
17	11	9	15

Which box plot displays the data shown in the chart? Circle the correct letter.

A.

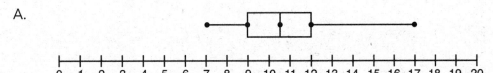

B.

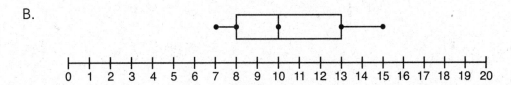

C.

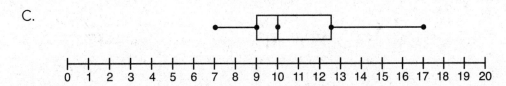

D.

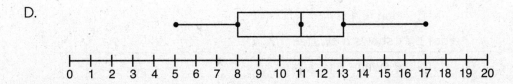

14. Consider the following data.

    74, 76, 84, 81, 79, 83, 87, 76

    What is the mean absolute deviation of the data set?

    _____

15. Denali would like to earn an A in math. Her average grade for the first four tests is 88%. What score must she earn on the final exam to increase her average to 90%? Explain your reasoning.

    _____

(Answers are on pages 258–263.)

CHAPTER 6

Practice Test 1

Computer Adaptive Test

Directions: On the actual Grade 6 Smarter Balanced exam, the instructions will inform you about the rules and navigation of the test. These instructions include the fact that you cannot skip questions and all questions on one page must be answered before moving on to the next page. In addition, you will be able to flag, or mark, a question to review later before submitting your test. Remember that the actual test is computer adaptive; this test is not.

1. Enter the exact difference.

$$63.817 - 19.45$$

2. What is the GCF of 18 and 36?

3. 30 is ⬜% of 50.

4. Enter a fraction that makes the equation true.

$$\frac{\square}{\square} \div \frac{3}{4} = \frac{1}{2}$$

5. Consider the statements in the table shown below. Select True or False for each statement.

Statement	True	False
The number −2 is located to the left of −7 on the number line.		
Both |−6| and −3 are located to the left of zero on the number line.		
9 is located to the right of −3.5 on the number line.		

6. Consider the following equation showing an example of the distributive property.

$$48 + 56 = 8(6 + \boxed{})$$

Enter the unknown value that makes the equation true.

7. 8 is located to the right of −3 on a horizontal number line. Enter an inequality that represents this statement.

8. Enter the value of $5^3 \cdot (17 - 14) + 49 \div 7$.

9. Select all the expressions that are equivalent to $8x + 12y$.

    A. $4(2x + 12y)$

    B. $2(4x + 6y)$

    C. $4(2x + 3y)$

    D. $5x + 3x + 2 + 6y$

    E. $x + 10y + 7x + 2y$

10. Complete the table for the inequality $x > -4$. Determine if each value of x makes the inequality true. Select True if the value is in the solution set of x. Select False if the value is not in the solution set of x.

Value of x	True	False
7		
-4.8		
0		
1.55		
-9		

11. Daniel saves the same amount of money each week as shown in the table below. Let *w* represent the number of weeks that Daniel saves. Let *t* represent the total amount of money saved, in dollars.

Number of Weeks, *w*	Total Amount Saved, *t*
1	$7
2	$14
3	$21
4	$28

Use the table above to determine whether each statement is true. Select True or False for each statement.

Statement	True	False
The equation *t* = 7 + *w* represents the relationship between the number of weeks and the total amount of money saved.		
The total amount saved is 7 times the number of weeks.		
The amount of money that Daniel saves depends on the number of weeks.		

12. Which of the following is NOT a statistical question?

A. What are the heights of the buildings in New York City?

B. How old are students in high school?

C. How often do middle school students eat pizza every year?

D. How many students are in your math class?

13. Consider this figure.

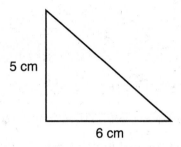

5 cm

6 cm

Enter the area of the right triangle in square centimeters.

Area = _____

14. The product of twelve and *n* is equal to 48. Enter the equation described in the sentence.

15. Use the fact that 17 × 356 = 6,052. Enter the exact product of 1.7 × 35.6.

16. Select all the ordered pairs that are located in the third quadrant of the coordinate plane.

A. (−5, −2)

B. (7, 1)

C. (−3, 4)

D. (6, −3)

E. (−2, −8)

17. Divide. Enter the exact quotient.

$$0.516 \div .24$$

18. The ABC Trucking Company uses 120 widgets every 3 hours. At this rate, how many widgets will they use in $4\frac{1}{2}$ hours?

19. Select the fraction that will complete the expression for converting 6 yards to inches.

$$\left(\frac{6\,\text{yards}}{1}\right) \times \left(\boxed{}\right) \times \left(\frac{12\,\text{inches}}{1\,\text{foot}}\right)$$

A. $\dfrac{1\,\text{yard}}{36\,\text{inches}}$

B. $\dfrac{3\,\text{feet}}{1\,\text{yard}}$

C. $\dfrac{1.2\,\text{feet}}{10\,\text{inches}}$

D. $\dfrac{120\,\text{yards}}{10\,\text{feet}}$

20. Carlos records the number of seconds that his friends each ran on the 100-yard dash.

15.2, 11.8, 12.9, 13.7, 14.6, 13.8, 12.7, 39.1, 13.2, 15.7, 14.8

Which number is an outlier?

21. What is the LCM of 6 and 10?

22. Trina has a parallelogram with a base of 8.5 centimeters and an area of 42.5 square centimeters. Find the height of Trina's parallelogram.

23. Show the expression $3(4x + 9)$ as a sum of two products.

24. Alan shaded 60% of his paper. If he shaded 12 equal-sized sections, how many equal-sized sections are on the paper?

25. Betty makes $4\frac{1}{4}$ cups of snack mix. She puts all the snack mix into smaller bags that can each hold $\frac{1}{4}$ cup. How many bags does Betty need?

26. The following table shows the number of miles 12 teachers travel to their school.

6	9	5	3
4	5	6	4
3	2	5	8

Find the mean absolute deviation for the data in the table.

27. Select all the equations that have $n = 8$ as a solution.

   A. $3 \cdot n = 11$

   B. $6 + n = 15$

   C. $n + 9 = 17$

   D. $n \cdot 5 = 40$

28. Bars of soap come in packages of 3 and 5. The 3-bar package of soap costs $2.89, and the 5-bar package costs $4.75. Which is the better deal? Explain your reasoning.

29. A rectangle has the following four coordinates:

Point A: (−3, 4)

Point B: (7, 4)

Point C: (7, −2)

Point D: (−3, −2)

Part A: On the grid below, plot and connect the four points to form rectangle ABCD. (Note: When you take the exam on computer, you will be told to use the Add Point and Connect Line tools.)

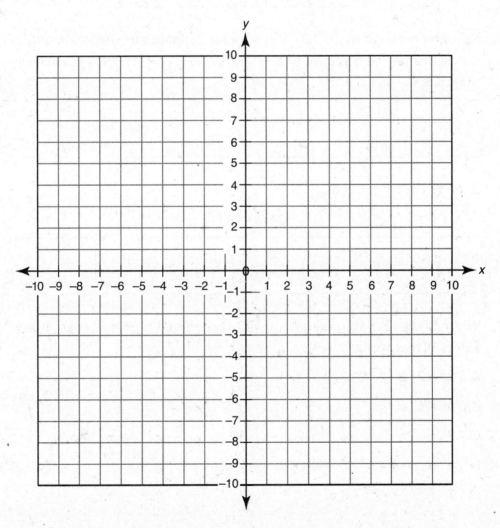

Part B: What is the distance between points C and D?

30. Use the following data to complete the table.

57, 29, 48, 65, 39, 40, 48, 67, 33, 80, 72, 48, 44, 91, 23

Median	
Lower Quartile	
Upper Quartile	
Interquartile Range	
Mode	

31. Consider the expression $3(3x + 3y)$. Lonnie simplifies the expression to $27xy$. Ivan simplifies the expression to $9x + 9y$. Who is correct? Why? Explain your reasoning.

32. Enter the exact quotient.

$$24\overline{)43,287}$$

33. Which of the following equations with exponential expressions are true? Select all that apply.

A. $2^4 = 2 \cdot 2 \cdot 2 \cdot 2 \cdot 2$

B. $6^2 = 6 \cdot 6$

C. $2^5 = 5 \cdot 5$

D. $6 \cdot 6 \cdot 6 \cdot 6 = 6^4$

E. $7 \cdot 7 \cdot 7 \cdot 7 \cdot 7 \cdot 7 = 6^7$

34. Enter the volume of the rectangular prism in cubic inches.

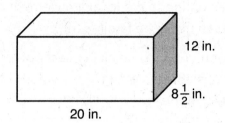

12 in.

$8\frac{1}{2}$ in.

20 in.

Volume = _____

35. Consider the following dot plot.

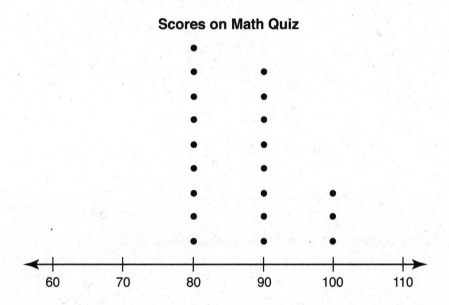

Determine whether each statement is true. Select True or False for each statement.

Statement	True	False
9 students scored 80 on their quiz.		
The mean score is 80.		
More than half of the class scored 90 or 100.		

(Answers are on pages 264–271.)

Performance Task

Ricky's family is planning an outing to the local amusement park. Answer each of the following six questions based upon the family's trip.

1. Rail cars at the amusement park are all in the shape of rectangular prisms. The base area of each car is 48 square feet. If the volume of one car is 456 cubic feet, find the height, h, of the car.

Consider the following wait times for different rides at the amusement park. Use this information to answer questions 2 and 3.

Wait Times

18	27	22	24
30	60	20	65
19	22	29	22
10	25	15	5

2. Find the median wait time for the sixteen rides listed.

3. Two of the longest waits for rides are 60 and 65 minutes. If both of those times were removed from the list, what would happen to the mean (increase, decrease, or stay the same)? Explain your reasoning.

4. In Ricky's family, there are 3 boys, 1 girl, and 2 parents. The cost of entrance into the amusement park is $37 for adults and $28 for children under 12. The children's ages are 10, 8, 7, and 3.

   Part A: Write an expression that identifies how much it would cost for Ricky's family to get into the amusement park.

   Part B: Solve the equation.

5. One of the roller coasters requires children, c, to be at least 40 inches tall to go on the ride. Write an inequality to represent this situation.

6. Ricky and his three siblings each order a $7.95 value meal for lunch. If his parents pay with two $20 bills, how much change will they get back?

(Answers are on pages 271–272.)

Practice Test 2

CHAPTER 7

Computer Adaptive Test

Directions: On the actual Grade 6 Smarter Balanced exam, the instructions will inform you about the rules and navigation of the test. These instructions include the fact that you cannot skip questions and all questions on one page must be answered before moving on to the next page. In addition, you will be able to flag, or mark, a question to review later before submitting your test. Remember that the actual test is computer adaptive; this test is not.

1. Multiply: 3.81×9.4

   Enter the exact product.

2. The following table contains equivalent ratios between x and y.

x	y
3	24
4	32
7	
9	72

   Fill in the missing value in the table.

3. Tina plays tennis every 5 days, and she goes to the gym to do yoga every 4 days. Today is Tuesday, October 3. Tina played tennis in the morning and did yoga in the afternoon. On what date will she do both activities again?

4. What is the GCF of 25 and 55?

5. The coordinate plane below shows the location of three different points.

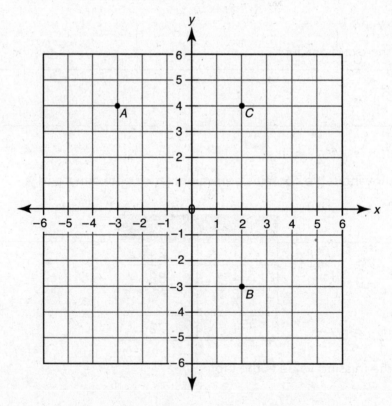

Enter the distance, in units, between point *B* and point *C*.

6. Select all the statements that correctly describe the expression $3^4 \cdot (4n - 12)$.

    A. The expression shows the product of two terms.

    B. The expression shows the sum of $4n - 12$.

    C. There are five terms in the expression.

    D. A term in the expression has a coefficient of 4.

7. What fraction makes the equation true?

$$\frac{3}{10} \div \frac{\Box}{\Box} = \frac{9}{10}$$

8. 20% of $\Box$ is 40.

9. Anthony can type 135 words in 3 minutes. How many words can Anthony type in 1 minute?

10. Select all the expressions that show a correct method to calculate 65% of 300.

   A. $\dfrac{65}{100} \times 300$

   B. $\dfrac{0.65}{100} \times 300$

   C. 0.65×300

   D. $\dfrac{65}{10} \times 300$

   E. 6.5×300

   ┌───┐
   │   │
   │   │
   │   │
   └───┘

11. Louie has some baseball cards. He traded for 62 more. He now has 107 baseball cards.

   Part A: Enter an equation to represent the number of baseball cards, c, that Louie had before he traded for 62 more.

   ┌───┐
   │   │
   │   │
   │   │
   └───┘

   Part B: Enter the number of cards represented by c in this situation.

   ┌───┐
   │   │
   │   │
   └───┘

12. Consider the following data set.

18, 15, 17, 19, 18, 18, 20, 14, 23, 18

Use the data set to complete the table. Select True or False for each statement.

Statement	True	False
The mode of the data is 23.		
The median of the data is 18.		
The mean of the data is 18.		
If another 18 was added to the data set, the mean would increase.		

13. Simplify: $2h + 3 + h + 4 + 2h$

14. Consider this figure.

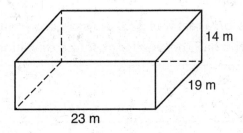

14 m

19 m

23 m

Enter the volume of the rectangular prism.

Volume = _____

15. The Chess Club is selling candy bars to raise money for their year-end field trip. The amount of money collected for each box of bars sold is the same. Let n represent the number of boxes sold. Let d represent the amount of money collected, in dollars.

Number of Boxes Sold, n	Amount of Money Collected in Dollars, d
1	
	50
3	75
4	100
8	

Part A: Fill in the table for all missing values of n and d.

Part B: Write an equation that represents the relationship between the number of boxes sold and the amount of money the Chess Club collected.

16. The average score on a test was 82%. Anissa's score was 78%, and Theodore's score was 91%. Who had the smaller absolute deviation from the mean?

17. The sixth-grade class at Williams Middle School designed a triangular playground behind their classroom.

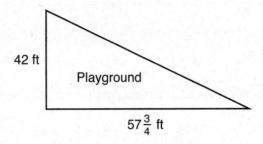

42 ft

Playground

$57\frac{3}{4}$ ft

Enter the area of the playground in square feet.

18. Which expression is equivalent to $\frac{3}{4} \div \frac{7}{8}$?

A. $\frac{3}{4} \cdot \frac{7}{8}$

B. $\frac{4}{3} \cdot \frac{7}{8}$

C. $\frac{4}{3} \cdot \frac{8}{7}$

D. $\frac{3}{4} \cdot \frac{8}{7}$

19. A submarine dove to a depth of 95 feet below the surface of the water. Enter the integer that represents the depth of the submarine.

20. Which number line shows the correct position of all the values shown?

$$-3, \frac{1}{4}, -1\frac{1}{2}, 2, 1\frac{3}{4}$$

A.

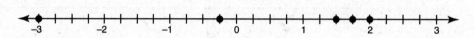

B.

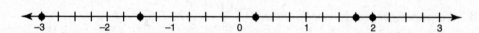

C.

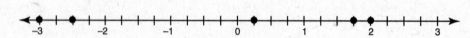

D.

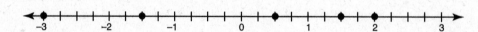

21. Select all the expressions that are equivalent to $4 + v + v + v + v$.

    A. $4v^4$

    B. $4 + 4v$

    C. $4 + v^4$

    D. $4(1 + v)$

22. Use the formula $A = \frac{1}{2}(b_1 + b_2) \times h$ to find the area of the trapezoid shown below.

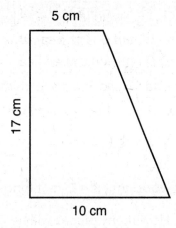

5 cm

17 cm

10 cm

Area = _____

23. Solve: $108 \div (13 + 5) \times 7$

24. Consider the following.

x	y
2	9
4	18
10	
12	54

Fill in the missing number to complete the table.

25. Consider the following statements in the table below. Select True or False for each statement.

Statement	True	False
The distance between –17 and 0 is the same as that between |–17| and 0 on the number line.		
On a number line, |7| and –7 are the same point.		
The distance between –8 and 0 on the number line is |8| units.		

26. Maddox has a piece of wood that is $4\frac{2}{3}$ feet long. He wants to cut it into several $1\frac{1}{6}$ foot pieces. How many pieces will he get?

27. Indicate the correct position for each number on the number line. Note that on the actual exam you will be asked to drag each number to its correct location on the number line using the dot below the number.

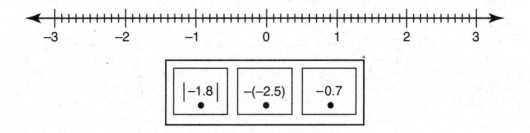

28. Enter the value of z that makes the equation true.

$$9z = 108$$

29. Matthew earns \$4 for every chore he does around his house. On Saturday, he completed some chores and earned a total of \$24.

Part A: Write an equation that shows the number of chores, c, Matthew completed on Saturday.

Part B: Solve for c in the previous equation.

30. Which is the correct box plot for the following data set?

3, 8, 11, 9, 7, 8, 2, 3, 5

A.

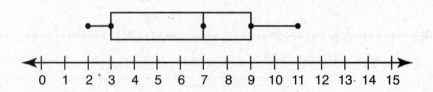

B.

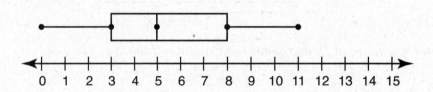

C.

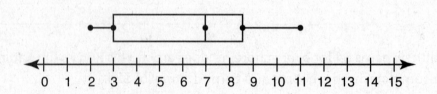

D.

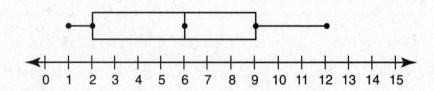

31. Enter the exact quotient: 1,846 ÷ 39

32. This coordinate grid represents the City of Gains-Ville. Each unit on the grid represents 1 square mile.

The movie theater is located at (5, 3).

The bank is located at (−2, 4).

A park is located at (5, −2).

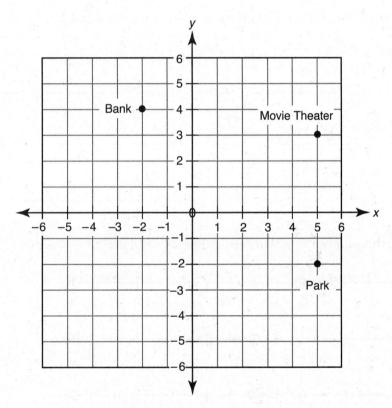

Enter the distance, in miles, from the park to the movie theater.

33. Sydney designed a small cereal box for a single-sized serving. The dimensions are given below.

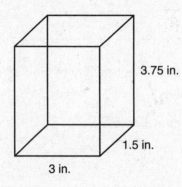

3.75 in.

1.5 in.

3 in.

How much cardboard is needed to make her cereal box?

34. Enter the value of $12y + 5 \cdot 6$ when $y = 3$.

35. Select the number line that represents all solutions of $m > -1\frac{1}{2}$.

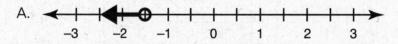

A.

B.

C.

D.

(Answers are on pages 272–281.)

Performance Task

Mr. Nunez has been looking to remodel his house. The house was built in 1956, and it has 2,000 square feet of living space. He would like to resurface all the floors. Recently, he has looked at some of the flooring options. Answer each of the following six questions based on the following three flooring options.

Smith's Flooring Company

Type of Flooring	Cost (per square foot)
Laminate	$2.82
Hardwood	$4.90
Bamboo	$6.25

The Arco Tile Company

Type of Flooring	Cost (per square foot)
Porcelain	$2.17
Ceramic	$4.70
Marble	$4.35

The Carrera Carpet Company

Type of Flooring	Cost (per square foot)
Berber	$4.25
Wool	$2.95
Shag	$3.80

1. Shag carpeting costs $3.80 per square foot. Fill in the missing value on the table.

Number of Square Feet	Cost
10	$38
20	$76
40	
60	$228
100	$380

2. Mr. Nunez would like to use ceramic tile floors in the entryway. The area of the entryway is 140 square feet. What is the total cost for the tile?

3. Mrs. Nunez would like to put porcelain (p) flooring in five of the rooms and wool (w) carpeting in the other three rooms. She writes the expression $w^3 + p^5$ to represent her flooring choices. Is this the correct expression? Why or why not?

4. The Nunez family has budgeted out at most $12,000 for the cost of the flooring.

   Part A: Write an inequality that represents the cost, c.

   Part B: Graph the inequality on a number line.

   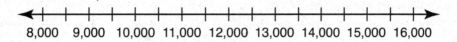

   8,000 9,000 10,000 11,000 12,000 13,000 14,000 15,000 16,000

5. One of the irregularly shaped rooms in the house is in the shape of a trapezoid.

   Part A: Use the formula $A = \frac{1}{2}(b_1 + b_2) \times h$ to find the area of that room.

   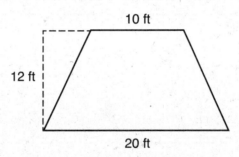

   10 ft

   12 ft

   20 ft

   Area = _____

   Part B: Find the cost if marble flooring is used for this room.

6. The Nunez family rounded each cost per square foot to the nearest dollar. The following lists the rounded values.

$$3, 5, 6, 2, 5, 4, 4, 3, 4$$

Part A: Find the median.

Part B: Find the mean.

Part C: Mr. Nunez thinks that the mode for the rounded values is 6. He reasons that since 6 is the largest value, it represents the mode. Do you agree with his reasoning? Why or why not? Explain your reasoning.

(Answers are on pages 281–283.)

Answers and Explanations

Chapter 1: Number Systems

Practice Exercises—Multi-Digit Division, page 17

1. **1,652R9**   Use the division steps in the chapter.

2. **760R2**   Use the division steps in the chapter.

3. **1,537**   Use the division steps in the chapter.

4. **817R47**   Use the division steps in the chapter.

5. **5,185**   Use the division steps in the chapter.

Practice Exercises—Greatest Common Factor and Least Common Multiple, pages 19–20

1. **5**   The largest number that goes into 25 and 90 without a remainder is 5.

2. **20**   The first multiple of 4 and 10 that is common to both is 20.

3. **17**   The largest number that goes into 17 and 68 without a remainder is 17.

4. **June 19**   The LCM for 6 and 9 is 18. 18 is the smallest number that is a multiple of both 6 and 9. If Becky braids her hair and paints her nails on June 1, she will do both 18 days later; 18 days after June 1 is June 19.

5. **4**   When factoring 48 and 60 with 12, you get $12 \times 4 = 48$ and $12 \times 5 = 60$.

Practice Exercises—Division of Fractions, pages 25–26

1. $\frac{9}{5}$ To find the reciprocal of any fraction, flip over the fraction so that the original numerator is now the denominator and the original denominator is now the numerator: $\frac{5}{9}$ becomes $\frac{9}{5}$.

2. $\frac{3}{14}$ First change the mixed number into an improper fraction. Keep the denominator the same. Multiply the whole number by the original denominator, and then add the original numerator. This will give you the new numerator. Then flip over the fraction to get its reciprocal:

$4\frac{2}{3} = \frac{14}{3}$ becomes $\frac{3}{14}$.

3. **4** $\frac{4}{5} \div \frac{1}{5} = \frac{4}{5} \times \frac{5}{1} = \frac{4}{1} = 4$

4. **34** $8\frac{1}{2} \div \frac{1}{4} = \frac{17}{2} \div \frac{1}{4} = \frac{17}{2} \times \frac{4}{1} = \frac{68}{2} = 34$

5. $\frac{7}{8}$ When the divisor is missing in a division of fractions problem, divide the dividend by the quotient to get the solution. If $a \div b = c$, then $a \div c = b$. So $\frac{2}{3} \div \frac{16}{21} = \frac{2}{3} \times \frac{21}{16} = \frac{42}{48} = \frac{7}{8}$.

6. $\frac{5}{24}$ When the dividend is missing in a division of fractions problem, multiply the quotient and the divisor together to get the solution. If $a \div b = c$, then $b \times c = a$. So $\frac{5}{6} \times \frac{1}{4} = \frac{5}{24}$.

7. **B** $\frac{5}{7} \div \frac{3}{8} = \frac{5}{7} \times \frac{8}{3}$. Remember to Keep, Change, and Flip. The first fraction, $\frac{5}{7}$, stays the same. The division sign is then changed into a multiplication sign. Last, flip over the second fraction so that it becomes its reciprocal.

Practice Exercises—Decimal Operations, pages 31–32

1. **245.77** After lining up the decimal points, subtract to find your solution.

2. **34.705** After adding a decimal point to 12 so that it becomes 12.0, line up your decimal points and add to find your solution.

3. **$2.58** Line up the decimal points and subtract. The difference is $2.58. Bob gave the cashier $50.00 (50.00 – 47.42 = 2.58).

4. **Yes** Add the price of the three sweaters: $12.99 + $12.95 + $13.50 = $39.44. Since Tammy has $40.00, she has enough money to purchase the sweaters.

5. ___ 0.25 – 0.90 is equal to –0.65.

   ___ 0.47 + 0.28 is equal to 0.75.

   x 0.3 + 0.35 is equivalent to 0.65 because you are adding 30 hundredths to 35 hundredths.

   x 0.39 + 0.26 is equivalent to 0.65.

   x 0.8 – 0.15 is equivalent to 0.65 because you are subtracting 15 hundredths from 80 hundredths.

6. **16.272** After multiplying 452 times 36, move the decimal point 3 places from right to left.

7. **17.2** Once you move the decimal point straight up from the dividend, divide the numbers until the answer terminates.

8. **155.77** There is one digit after each decimal point in the problem. Move the decimal point 2 places from right to left in the answer.

9. **7.125** Since you are given the entire area of the rectangular garden, which is 34.2 square feet, you must find the missing length. The area for a rectangle can be found by multiplying the length times the width. In this case, you divide 34.2 ÷ 4.8 to get your solution.

10. **31.5** Move the decimal point two places to the right in the divisor (0.04) and the dividend (1.26). Since 4 does not go into 126 evenly, you will have to add a zero to the end of the dividend (1.260). Once you have moved the decimal point to the right two places, place the decimal point straight up in your quotient. The quotient is 31.5.

Practice Exercises—Rational Numbers on a Number Line and Absolute Value, pages 36–37

1. **-7, -4, -2, 0, |-3|, |-5|** Since –7 is the farthest from zero on the left, it is the smallest. It is followed by –4 and then –2. The next integer is 0. It is followed by the two absolute values. |–3| equals 3. The largest value is |–5| because it equals 5.

2.

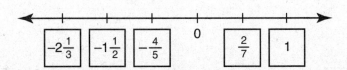

This is the order the numbers follow from left to right (from least to greatest).

3.

Statement	True	False	Reason
5 is located to the right of |−8|.		X	5 is located to the left of |−8| because |−8| = 8.
The opposite of the opposite of −4 = 4.		X	The opposite of −4 is 4, but the opposite of 4 is −4.
−|9| = −9.	X		|9| = 9. A negative sign in front of the absolute value symbol means that you take the opposite of that value. The opposite of 9 is −9.

4. **12**   The opposite of a number is the same rational number but on the opposite side of zero on the number line. −12 and +12 are opposites because they are the same integer and the same distance from zero but on opposite sides of zero.

5. **2, 0, −1.5, −2, −3**   This is the order that the numbers follow from right to left (greatest to least) on the number line.

Practice Exercises—Graphing Points on a Coordinate Plane, pages 42–43

1. **C (−3, 1) and E (−5, 2)**   Both C and E are located in Quadrant II because the x-values are negative and the y-values are positive.

2. **A (6, −5)** could be dragged or indicated at the point in Quadrant IV. The x-value is positive and the y-value is negative.

   B (−6, −5) could be dragged or indicated at the point in Quadrant III. Both the x-value and the y-value are negative.

   C (−6, 5) could be dragged or indicated at the point in Quadrant II. The x-value is negative and the y-value is positive.

3.

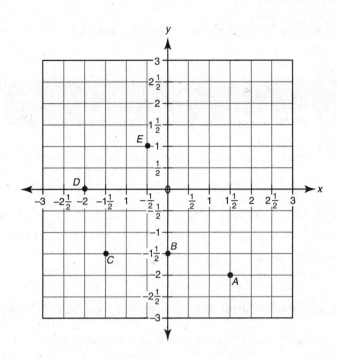

Practice Exercises—Distance, pages 45–47

1. **7**   Count from one point to the other on the coordinate plane to find the distance. Another way to find the distance is by using absolute value. The distance between point *A* at (3, −2) and point *B* at (3, 5) is 7 because |−2| + |5| = 7. Add their absolute values because the ordered pairs are in different quadrants.

2. **6**   Plot both points, and count from one point to the other. Another way to find the distance is by using absolute value. The distance between (−7, −3) and (−1, −3) is 6 because |−7| − |−1| = 6. Subtract their absolute values because the ordered pairs are in the same quadrant.

3. Part A. **|−3| + |5|**   Add the absolute values because the two points are in different quadrants. Ignore the *y*-values because they are the same.

   Part B. **|−3| + |5| = 3 + 5 = 8**. The absolute value of all numbers is positive because absolute value measures a number's distance from zero.

4. **Bailey is correct because the distance is 5.** The distance between two points in the same quadrant is the difference between the absolute values of the *x*- or *y*-values that are different. The points (−4, 6) and (−4, 1) are both in Quadrant II. Their *y*-values are different. To find the distance between the two points, take the absolute value of 6 and subtract the absolute value of 1. The distance between the two points is 5.

Practice Exercises—Reflections, pages 49-50

1.

Original Point	Coordinates of Point After Reflection Over x-axis
(7, -5)	(7, 5)
(-3, 1)	(-3, -1)

2. **IV** The reflection of a point in Quadrant III over the y-axis (vertical axis) is found in Quadrant IV. In this case, the x-value of the original point, −4, would change to 4. The reflection point is (4, −2).

Practice Review Test—Number Systems, pages 51-55

1. **538.68** Line up the decimal points and then subtract.

2. **5** When using the distributive property, $12 \times 5 = 60$ and $12 \times 6 = 72$.

3. **16.472** Since there is one number to the right of the decimal point in 2.9 and two numbers to the right of the decimal in 5.68, there will be a total of three numbers to the right of the decimal in your product. Another way to check your solution is by multiplying $3 \times 6 = 18$ to find an approximate answer. Then, 16.472 is the only solution close to 18. This estimation process works when you multiply mixed numbers.

4. **444R40** This is the quotient after dividing 66 into 29,344.

5. **−9** The opposite of −9 is +9. When you take the opposite of +9, you are right back at −9.

6. **25** This is the greatest factor that goes into both 50 and 75 evenly without a remainder.

7. $\frac{3}{4}$ To find the solution, divide $\frac{1}{3} \div \frac{4}{9}$ and then simplify.

8. **0.9 − 0.19 and 0.6 + 0.11** These are the solutions that subtract or add to 0.71. Remember to line up the decimal points when you add or subtract decimals.

9.

Statement	True	False	Reason
The number –8 is located to the right of 10 on the number line.		X	–8 is not located to the right of 10 because all negative numbers are to the left of all positive numbers on the number line.
The number –7 is located to the right of –15 on the number line.	X		–7 is located to the right of –15 because –7 is closer to 0.
|–7.9| is located to the left of 7.45 on the number line.		X	|–7.9| is not located to the left of 7.45 because its true value is +7.9. When comparing 7.9 to 7.45, 7.9 is located to the right of 7.45 because it has a greater value.

10. **18**   This is the smallest number that is a multiple of both 6 and 9. It is the third multiple of 6 and the second multiple of 9.

11. **A and C**   Both (–3, 8) and (–4, 1) are in Quadrant II. They each have a negative x-value and a positive y-value.

12.

Number	True	False	Reason
|–10|		X	The absolute value of –10 is equal to 10, which is not less than 9.
7	X		7 is less than 9.
$-5\frac{7}{8}$	X		Any negative whole number, fraction, or mixed number is less than 9.
–(–12)		X	The opposite of –12 is +12. Obviously, 12 is greater than 9.

13. **C** $\frac{7}{9} \times \frac{6}{5}$ shows the appropriate expression for changing division into multiplication with the proper use of a reciprocal. Only the second fraction changes to its reciprocal after changing the division sign to a multiplication sign.

14. **0.28** This is the correct solution after dividing 0.05 into 0.014.

15. **−4.2 > −10.** If a number is to the right of −10 on the number line, that number is greater than −10 because it is closer to zero.

16. **−5, −3.4, −2.8, −$\frac{3}{4}$, 0** The smallest number is −5 because it is farthest to the left on the number line. As the numbers move farther to the right, they become larger. The largest number in this list is 0. It is farthest to the right on the number line.

17. **No. The distance is 11.** Add the absolute values when finding the distance between two points in different quadrants. $|7| + |-4| = 11$

18.

Coordinate Points	New Coordinate Point After Reflection Across the y-axis
(−4, 5)	(4, 5)
(−3, −2)	(3, −2)

When reflecting a point across the y-axis, the x-value changes to its opposite. The x-value changes because a reflection across the y-axis is a horizontal change.

Chapter 2: Ratios and Proportional Thinking

Practice Exercises—Ratios, page 58

1. $\frac{5 \text{ bears}}{7 \text{ lions}}$, **5:7, or 5 to 7** Since the relationship is between bears and lions, bears are listed first and lions are listed second in the ratio.

2. $\frac{4 \text{ tigers}}{3 \text{ cheetahs}}$, **4:3, or 4 to 3** Since the relationship is between tigers and cheetahs, tigers are listed first and cheetahs are listed second in the ratio. Remember that a ratio is not a fraction, so you do not change the improper ratio into a mixed number.

3. $\frac{7 \text{ lions}}{19 \text{ all animals}}$, **7:19, or 7 to 19** The relationship calls for the ratio of lions to all the animals. There are 7 lions and 19 total animals. Make sure that when you add all the animals, you include the lions.

4. **Part to whole ratio**   The relationship is a part to whole ratio because you are comparing a portion (bears and cheetahs) to the total amount (all the animals).

5. $\frac{7}{25}$, **7:25, or 7 to 25**   The relationship asks for the ratio of misspelled words to the total amount of words. Since there are 18 words spelled correctly, the number of words spelled incorrectly is 7. Gladys misspelled 7 of the 25 words on her spelling test.

Practice Exercises—Rates, pages 61-62

1. **18 hot dogs**   If Paul eats 3 hot dogs in 15 minutes, he will eat more hot dogs in an hour and a half. One way to find the solution is by setting up a proportion and solving:

$$\frac{3 \text{ hot dogs}}{15 \text{ minutes}} = \frac{? \text{ hot dogs}}{90 \text{ minutes}}$$

The multiplier between 15 and 90 is 6. If you then multiply 3 × 6, you will get 18. A great way to check your solution is by cross multiplying: 90 × 3 = 270 and 15 × 18 = 270. When cross products are equivalent, the ratios are equivalent.

2. **1,200 words**   Preston types 50 words per minute. To find out how many words he can type in 24 minutes, multiply 50 × 24.

3. **12 minutes**   Ronald takes 2 minutes to run around the track once, because 8 ÷ 4 = 2. Since Ronald now runs 6 times around the track, multiply 6 × 2 = 12.

4. **432 pieces**   Since Jade and Holly use 72 pieces to build every model airplane, multiply 72 × 6 = 432.

5. **14 baskets**   You need to look at the minutes to solve the problem. The minutes go from 6 to 1.5. This uses a divisor of 4. If you then divide 4 into 56, the solution comes to 14.

Practice Exercises—Unit Rate and Unit Price, pages 65-66

1. $\frac{32 \text{ pages}}{1 \text{ night}}$ To find the unit rate, divide both the numerator and denominator by the denominator. The original rate is 96 pages in 3 nights.

$$\frac{96 \text{ pages}}{3 \text{ nights}} \div \frac{3}{3} = \frac{32 \text{ pages}}{1 \text{ night}}$$

2.

	$0.45 for 1 pound of grapes
X	$12.00 for 15 pounds of grapes
	$16.00 for 18 pounds of grapes
X	$2.00 for $2\frac{1}{2}$ pounds of grapes
X	$0.80 for 1 pound of grapes

Set up all the problems as equivalent rates. You can then cross multiply or can check with a multiplier or divisor to see if they are equivalent.

Not equivalent: $\dfrac{\$4.00}{5 \text{ pounds}} \neq \dfrac{\$0.45}{1 \text{ pound}}$

These are not equivalent rates because $5 \div 5 = 1$ but $\$4.00 \div 5 = \$0.80$ and not 0.45.

Equivalent: $\dfrac{\$4.00}{5 \text{ pounds}} \times \dfrac{3}{3} = \dfrac{\$12.00}{15 \text{ pounds}}$

These two rates are equivalent because their cross products are equal: $4 \times 15 = 60$ and $5 \times 12 = 60$. The multiplier of 3 is used to prove they are equivalent.

Not equivalent: $\dfrac{\$4.00}{5 \text{ pounds}} \times \dfrac{4}{4} \neq \dfrac{\$16.00}{18 \text{ pounds}}$

These two rates are not equivalent when the multiplier of 4 is used: $4 \times 4 = 16$ but $5 \times 4 \neq 18$. You can also use cross multiplication to prove that the two rates are not equivalent: $4 \times 18 = 72$ but $5 \times 16 = 80$.

Equivalent: $\dfrac{\$4.00}{5 \text{ pounds}} \div \dfrac{2}{2} = \dfrac{\$2.00}{2\frac{1}{2} \text{ pounds}}$

These two rates are equivalent, because a divisor of 2 can be used to get from one rate to another. Their cross products are also equivalent: $4 \times 2.5 = 10$ and $5 \times 2 = 10$.

Equivalent: $\dfrac{\$4.00}{5 \text{ pounds}} \div \dfrac{5}{5} = \dfrac{\$0.80}{1 \text{ pound}}$

These two rates are equivalent, because a divisor of 5 can be used to get from one rate to another. The answer in this problem is the unit rate. Both of their cross products are also equivalent: $4 \times 1 = 4$ and $5 \times 0.8 = 4$.

3. **$71.50** Find the unit rate by dividing. Then multiply 11 times the unit rate per hour. To find the unit rate, divide your initial rate by 5.

$$\dfrac{\$32.50}{5 \text{ hours}} \div \dfrac{5}{5} = \dfrac{\$6.50}{1 \text{ hour}}$$

Once you have the unit rate, multiply that rate by 11. $6.5 \times 11 = \$71.50$.

4. **$7.00 per candle**   To find the unit rate, divide the initial rate by 6. You are trying to find the cost per candle. So you need to divide the rate by the number of candles.

$$\frac{\$42.00}{6 \text{ candles}} \div \frac{6}{6} = \frac{\$7.00}{1 \text{ candle}}$$

5. **3 movies per month**   If Warren watches 18 movies in 6 months, divide both numbers by 6 to find the unit rate.

$$\frac{18 \text{ movies}}{6 \text{ months}} \div \frac{6}{6} = \frac{3 \text{ movies}}{1 \text{ month}}$$

Practice Exercises—Tables of Equivalent Ratios, pages 68–69

1.

Boys	Girls
2	3
4	6
6	9
8	12
14	21

The missing value of 2, in the top box on the left, comes from the original ratio of 2:3 boys to girls. To find the missing number in the right column next to the 4, multiply 3 × 2. You will perform this operation because the number of boys is also being multiplied by 2 to go from 2 (in the first row) to 4 (in the second row). To find the missing value in the right column next to 8, there are a few numbers you could use. Since there are 4 boys to 6 girls, you can double 6: 4 × 2 = 8, so 6 × 2 = 12.

2.

7	56
9	72
11	88
13	104

You can find the missing number of 72 by using a multiplier of 8. The pattern shows that all the other ratios increase by a multiplier of 8: 7 × 8 = 56, 11 × 8 = 88, and 13 × 8 = 104. You can then multiply 9 × 8 to get your solution of 72.

3.

Number of Apps	Total Cost
3	$4.50
6	**$9.00**
9	$13.50
12	**$18.00**
20	$30.00

The missing number can be found by using a multiplier of 1.5 because that is the relationship comparing the number of apps to total cost. You can also use the fact that the number of apps doubles from 3 to 6. The total cost therefore also doubles from $4.50 to $9.00. The number of apps also doubles from 6 to 12. The total cost therefore also doubles from $9.00 to $18.00.

4.

Number of hours	2	6	8	12	20
Number of miles	14	**42**	56	**84**	**140**

The number of hours to miles uses a multiplier of 7: $6 \times 7 = 42$, $12 \times 7 = 84$, and $20 \times 7 = 140$.

Practice Exercises—Graphing Ratios, pages 71–72

1. Part A.

Candy (lb)	Price per Pound
1	$2.50
2	$5.00
3	**$7.50**
4	$10.00

The missing value is $7.50. Each pound of candy costs $2.50. Multiply the number of pounds by $2.50 to get your solution.

Part B. **Points should be placed at (1, $2.50); (2, $5.00); (3, $7.50); and (4, $10.00).**

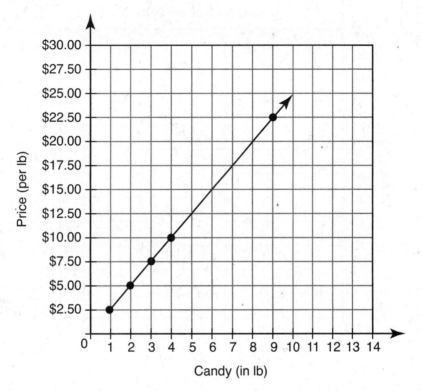

Part C. **$22.50** Since each pound costs $2.50, multiply 9 × 2.50 to get the solution.

2. Part A.

Number of Coffee Tables	1	2	4	7
Time (hours)	6	12	24	42

The missing value for coffee tables is 4. The two missing values for time are 12 and 42. Each coffee table takes 6 hours to make. Multiply the number of coffee tables by 6 to get the total amount of time. In the third box, divide 24 by 6 to get 4.

Part B. **The four ordered pairs are (1, 6); (2, 12); (4, 24); and (7, 42).**

Part C. **Points should be placed at (1, 6); (2, 12); (4, 24); and (7, 42).**

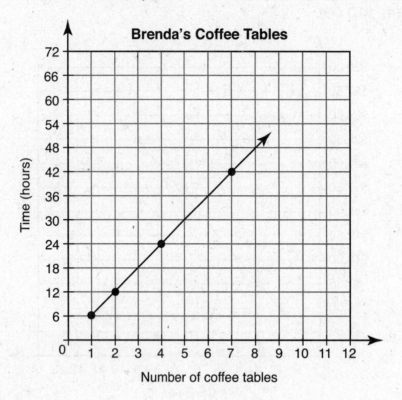

Brenda's Coffee Tables

Number of coffee tables

Practice Exercises—Percent, page 76

1. **40** 100% of any number is that original number.

2. **20%** Raul made 80% of the free throws.

$$\frac{16}{20} \times \frac{5}{5} = \frac{80}{100}$$

$$\frac{80}{100} = 80\%$$

Since Raul made 80% of the free throws, he missed 20%.

3. **320** Brian read 80 pages, which is 25% of the total number of pages in the book. This means that he still needs to read 75% of the book. One way to solve this is by writing and solving an equation. Let p equal the number of pages in the book.

$$0.25p = 80$$

$$\frac{0.25p}{0.25} = \frac{80}{0.25}$$

$$p = 320$$

4. **8.04** One way to solve this problem is by changing the percent to a decimal and multiplying.

$$12\% = 0.12$$

$$
\begin{array}{r}
1 \\
0.12 \\
\times\ 67 \\
\hline
84 \\
+\ 720 \\
\hline
8.04
\end{array}
$$

5. **87.5%** This is a division problem. Divide $7 \div 8$.

$$
\begin{array}{r}
0.875 \\
8\overline{)7.00}
\end{array}
$$

To change a decimal to a percent, move the decimal point two places to the right: $0.875 = 87.5\%$.

Practice Exercises—Measurement Conversions, page 79

1.   **6** Use the following conversion to reach the solution.

$$\left(\frac{96\ \cancel{\text{ounces}}}{1}\right) \times \left(\frac{1\ \text{pound}}{16\ \cancel{\text{ounces}}}\right) = \frac{96\ \text{pounds}}{16} = 6\ \text{lb}$$

The reason that you use pounds over ounces in your second ratio is to eliminate the ounces.

2. **2.5** Use the following conversion to reach the solution.

$$\left(\frac{30\ \cancel{\text{inches}}}{1}\right) \times \left(\frac{1\ \text{foot}}{12\ \cancel{\text{inches}}}\right) = \frac{30\ \text{feet}}{12} = 2.5\ \text{feet}$$

The second ratio must include feet over inches. This will help you cancel out the inches.

3. **3** There are 3 feet in every yard.

4. **16** There are 16 ounces in every pound.

5. **2.5** Since there are 4 quarts in every gallon, 10 quarts are equivalent to 2.5 gallons.

Practice Review Test—Ratios and Proportional Thinking, pages 80–85

1. **80** Using equivalent fractions is one of the many ways that you can find your solution. Remember that when a fraction has 100 as the denominator, the numerator is the identified percent in that fraction. $\frac{16}{20} \times \frac{5}{5} = \frac{80}{100} = 80\%$

2.

x	y
3	9
5	15
7	21
9	27

The y-value when x = 5 is 15. The x-value when y = 27 is 9. You can multiply the x-value by 3 to get the y-value. You can divide the y-value by 3 to get the x-value.

3. **142** There are many ways to find the value. However, using equivalent ratios will help you to see the relationship: $\frac{71}{n} = \frac{50}{100}$. Once you write the equation, cross multiply. The result of this is 50n = 7,100. After dividing 7,100 by 50, the solution comes out to 142.

4. **62.5%** You can use division to find the decimal: $8\overline{)5.000}$ (= .625). Since every percent is out of one hundred, move your decimal point two places to the right: 0.625 = 62.5%.

5. **12.5 hours** Using the unit rate can help you find the number of hours.

$$\frac{120 \text{ shirts}}{5 \text{ hours}} \div \frac{5}{5} = \frac{24 \text{ shirts}}{1 \text{ hour}}$$

You can then use this unit rate to find the number of hours needed to clean 300 shirts: $24\overline{)300}$ (= 12.5).

6. **18 problems per hour** Reduce the initial rate given by using division.

$$\frac{126 \text{ problems}}{7 \text{ hours}} \div \frac{7}{7} = \frac{18 \text{ problems}}{1 \text{ hour}}$$

7.

Number of Pages	4	8	24	48
Number of Minutes	10	20	60	120

The unit rate is 2.5 pages per minute. You can get this by dividing 20 by 8. You can also use the multiplier of 2.5 throughout your table to go from pages to minutes.

8. **The better buy is the 16-ounce can.**   The 16-ounce can costs $0.13 per ounce after dividing, and the 12-ounce can costs $0.14 per can after dividing and rounding.

9. **$10.80**   To find the amount of the tip, multiply 72 times 0.15. Another way to compute the tip is to find 10% of the number, which is $7.20, and add it to 5% of the number, which is $3.60.

10. **37.2**   Multiply 0.30 × 124 to get the solution.

11.

Tickets	1	2	3	4
Total Cost	12	24	36	48

The unit rate is $12 per ticket. This rate can be used to fill in the table. You can also multiply the tickets by 12 to get the total cost. You can divide the total cost by 12 to get the tickets.

12.

	2 + 3
X	3 to 2
	2:3
X	$\frac{3}{2}$
	3 − 2
X	3:2

The ratios of 3:2, 3 to 2, and $\frac{3}{2}$ are all correct. They identify dogs to cats. Be careful with this problem. The introductory information gives cats to dogs. However, the question switches the order and asks for dogs to cats.

13. **89**   Whenever you have 100% of any number, the solution is that number.

14. **15**   Multiply 4 forks by 5 to get 20. Therefore, 3 spoons multiplied by 5 equals 15.

$$\frac{3 \text{ spoons}}{4 \text{ forks}} = \frac{15 \text{ spoons}}{20 \text{ forks}}$$

15. **C and D**   The expression 0.45 × 320 correctly shows 45% changed to a decimal. The expression $\frac{45}{100}$ × 320 correctly illustrates 45% changed to a fraction.

16. **15** The multiplier is 2.5. You can again set up this problem as a proportion with two equivalent ratios. Then find the missing value.

$$\frac{6 \text{ miles}}{4 \text{ hours}} = \frac{? \text{ miles}}{10 \text{ hours}}$$

One way is to simplify $\frac{6 \text{ miles}}{4 \text{ hours}} \div \frac{2}{2} = \frac{3 \text{ miles}}{2 \text{ hours}}$. Once you have done this, you can see that $2 \times 5 = 10$. So 3×5 gives you the solution of 15 miles.

17. **80%** A total of 40 students were surveyed; 32 out of the 40 did not choose ice cream as their favorite dessert. Change the fraction $\frac{32}{40}$ to a decimal by dividing.

$$40\overline{)32.0}^{.8}$$

0.8 is the same as 0.80 or eighty-hundredths, and 80 out of 100 is equivalent to 80%.

18. Part A. $\frac{3 \text{ rectangles}}{4 \text{ triangles}}$, **3:4**, or **3 to 4**

    Part B. $\frac{5 \text{ circles and rectangles}}{9 \text{ total shapes}}$, **5:9**, or **5 to 9**

    Part C. **Part to whole ratio** Anytime the second part of the ratio includes all of the objects or things in the problem, it is a part to whole ratio.

19. **There are 3 feet in every yard.**

Feet: **3**
Yards: **1**
Inches: **126**

20. Part A.

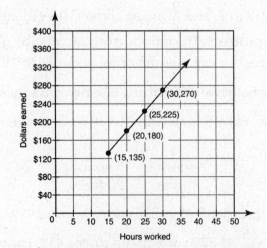

Part B.   **40 hours**   If you extend the line on the graph, it will go through (40, 360). The multiplier in the problem is 9: $40 \times 9 = 360$.

21.   **32.5 gallons per minute**   When finding the unit rate, divide both numbers in your rate by the denominator.

$$\frac{325 \text{ gallons}}{10 \text{ minutes}} \div \frac{10}{10} = \frac{32.5 \text{ gallons}}{1 \text{ minute}}$$

Chapter 3: Expressions and Equations

Practice Exercises—Exponents, pages 89-90

1.   **32** $2^5 = 2 \times 2 \times 2 \times 2 \times 2 = 32$

2.   **$n \times n \times n$**   Since you are not given a numeric value for n, the only thing you can do is to expand the expression. $n^3 = n \times n \times n$

3.   **11.391** $1.5^6 = 1.5 \times 1.5 \times 1.5 \times 1.5 \times 1.5 \times 1.5 = 11.391$

4.   **Tabitha's flaw is that she added 2 + 2 + 2 + 2 = 8.**

$$2^4 = 2 \times 2 \times 2 \times 2 = 16$$

5.   **B, D, and E** 5^4 is equivalent to 625. Both $5 \times 5 \times 5 \times 5$ and $5 \times 25 \times 5$ are also equivalent to 5^4.

Practice Exercises—Order of Operations, pages 91-92

1.   **6**   First calculate 3 raised to the second power. Then multiply 5×4. Last, you proceed from left to right: $17 + 9 - 20 = 6$.

2.   **113**   First you perform the two operations in the parentheses, squaring the exponent first: $5^2 + 9 = 34$. Then you divide 6 into 24. Last, proceed from left to right: $83 - 4 + 34 = 113$.

3.   **33**   First divide 3 into 18. Then add $27 + 6 = 33$.

4.   **39**   First solve the exponential power of $3^3 = 27$. Then divide 10 into 30. Once you have only addition and subtraction remaining, solve from left to right: $15 + 27 - 3 = 39$.

5.   **42**   First work out the addition in the parentheses first. Then solve the exponential power of $9^2 = 81$. Next divide 7 into 21, and multiply that quotient by 13. Finally, $81 - 39 = 42$.

Practice Exercises—Identifying Parts of an Expression, page 94

1.

	Number of Terms	Coefficient(s)	Constant(s)
$5x + 7$	2	5	7
$0.5x - 12$	2	0.5	-12
$2x + 6 - 3y$	3	2 and -3	6

2. **18**   The constant is a numerical term without any variable attached to it. It never changes in value.

3. **2**   Terms are separated by plus or minus signs. Although there are quite a few variables, the expression contains only two terms because there is only one plus sign.

4. **9**   The coefficient is the number in front of a variable. It tells you how many groups of that variable you have. Since 9 is in front of the y in the term $9y$, it is considered the coefficient of y.

Practice Exercises—Writing and Solving Expressions, page 97

1. **$n - 9$**   The order matters. You are taking 9 from a number, so the variable goes first.

2. **$2(6 + n)$**   You are doubling a sum. The sum must be in parentheses so you will perform that operation first.

3. **$4n$**   You have 4 groups of n because the word *product* represents the answer in multiplication.

4. **2**   Substitute the given values for y and x: $12\left(\dfrac{1}{2}\right) = 6$ and $6 - 4 = 2$. Multiply before you subtract. The letter z is a distractor in the problem and is not needed.

5. **108**   The expression $12c$ is the same as 12 groups of c. Since $c = 9$, you have 12 groups of 9, which is equivalent to 108.

Practice Exercises—Distributive Property and Equivalent Expressions, page 100

1. **$2x + 4y - 9$**   You can combine only the x-values because they are like terms.

2. **$8x - 20y$**   Based on the distributive property, 4 groups of $2x - 5y$ is equivalent to $8x - 20y$.

3. **$8(3s + 4t)$**   The GCF for 24 and 32 is 8. When you factor out 8 groups from $24s + 32t$, the result is $8(3s + 4t)$.

4. **7** The right side adds up to 119. If you plug in 7 and multiply it by the sum of (8 + 9), you also get 119.

5. **B, D, and E** Choice A is wrong because $2(4x + 16) = 8x + 32$ after you distribute and multiply 2 by both terms inside the parentheses. Choice B is correct because $8(x + 2) = 8x + 16$ after you distribute and multiply 8 times x and 8 times 2. Choice C is incorrect because $4x + 4 + 12 = 4x + 16$ after you add the like terms. Choice D is correct because $(2x + 4)4 = 8x + 16$ after you distribute and multiply 4 times $2x$ and 4 times 4. Just because the 4 is after the parentheses does not mean that you don't distribute the 4 times both terms inside the parentheses. Choice E is correct because $10x - 3x + x + 16 = 8x + 16$ after you combine the x-terms. When a variable is all by itself without a coefficient, the actual coefficient for that variable is 1.

Practice Exercises—Writing and Solving Equations, pages 103–104

1. $\frac{n}{12}$ **= 10 and** n **= 120** The word "is" represents the equals sign, which separates the two expressions.

2. x **= 8.5** Use the inverse property of dividing by 5 to solve the equation.

3. $\frac{3}{4}$ **+** s **=** $1\frac{1}{2}$ **and** s **=** $\frac{3}{4}$ Kate starts with $\frac{3}{4}$ of a cup of sugar, but she needs to add $\frac{3}{4}$ cup more until she gets $1\frac{1}{2}$ cups of sugar.

4. **B and D** In choice B, 7 groups of 5 is equivalent to 35. In choice D, 9 groups of 5 is equivalent to 45.

5. n **= 5** To isolate the variable, you must divide both sides by 3.5.

$$3.5n = 17.5$$
$$\frac{3.5n}{3.5} = \frac{17.5}{3.5}$$
$$n = 5$$

Practice Exercises—Inequalities, pages 110–112

1.

Value of x	True	False
−4.2		X
|−7|	X	
$-1\frac{1}{4}$	X	
−3.9		X

Any number that is to the right of –3 on the number line would make the inequality $x > -3$ true.

2. **$m \geq 2,500$** Ana must make 2,500 or more to afford the car. The inequality symbol has a line to show that the inequality includes 2,500.

3. Part A. **$x > 42$** Use the inverse property to solve the inequality. So add 19 to both sides of the inequality. Any number that is greater than 42 makes the inequality true.

   Part B. **The number line will include an open circle at 42 with an arrow pointing to the right.**

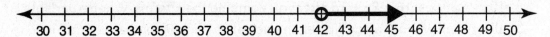

Value of x	True	False
-2		X
12	X	
0		X
8	X	

A good way to look at an inequality is by making sure the variable is on the left side. For this inequality, switch everything so that it reads $x > 7$. This means that all the numbers that are greater than 7 will make the inequality true. Since 12 and 8 are greater than 7, they are true. However, 0 and –2 are less than 7 and are therefore false.

5. Part A. **$m \leq \$20.00$** The words "at most" mean that $20.00 is the most he can spend. Tommy can spend $20.00 or less than $20.00.

   Part B. **The number line will include a closed circle at 20 with an arrow pointing to the left.**

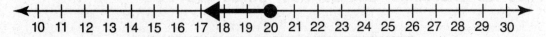

6. **D** When graphing an inequality on a number line, it is a good idea to switch any inequalities when the variable is on the right side. So $-4 < n$ should be switched to $n > -4$. When the variable is on the left, the direction the inequality is pointing is the direction you will draw your arrow.

Practice Exercises—Independent and Dependent Variables, page 113

1. Part A. **The independent variable is the number of churros sold.** The number of churros sold is not affected by the money earned.

   Part B. **The dependent variable is the money earned from the sale of the churros.** The amount earned depends on how many churros are sold.

   Part C. **$d = 0.50c$** The unit rate of $0.50 per churro is multiplied by the number of churros to show how much money is earned.

Practice Review Test—Expressions and Equations, pages 114–118

1.

Less than 20	Between 20 and 100	Greater than 100
4^2	2.2^4	5^3
$\left(\frac{1}{6}\right)^4$	7^2	3^5

Less than 20:
$$4^2 = 4 \times 4 = 16$$
$$\left(\frac{1}{6}\right)^4 = \frac{1}{6} \times \frac{1}{6} \times \frac{1}{6} \times \frac{1}{6} = \frac{1}{1,296}$$

Between 20 and 100:
$$7^2 = 7 \times 7 = 49$$
$$2.2^4 = 2.2 \times 2.2 \times 2.2 \times 2.2 = 23.4256$$

Greater than 100:
$$5^3 = 5 \times 5 \times 5 = 125$$
$$3^5 = 3 \times 3 \times 3 \times 3 \times 3 = 243$$

2. Part A. **−18** The constant is −18 because −18 does not change in the expression.

   Part B. **3 and 7** The coefficients are 3 and 7 because they identify the number of groups of the variables.

   Part C. **3** There are 3 terms in the expression because they are separated by the two + or − signs.

3. **12 + 9(x − 1)** Kendrell downloaded 12 apps on the first day, when $x = 1$. He then added 9 more downloads every day after that. Since you don't know

the number of days, multiply 9 times the number of days minus the first day ($x - 1$) to get the total number of downloads after day 1. Then add that to the downloads from day 1.

4. **35** First substitute the 7 and the 4 for each corresponding variable. Perform the multiplication within the parentheses and then the addition within the parentheses. Next, calculate the value of the term containing the exponent. Finally, subtract the numbers to find the value of the expression.

$$3^4 - (6x + y)$$
$$3^4 - (6(7) + 4)$$
$$3^4 - (42 + 4)$$
$$3^4 - (46)$$
$$81 - 46$$
$$35$$

5. **No** When distributing, you must multiply the outside term by all the terms on the inside. Joshua did not distribute the 3×12. The correct answer is $12x + 36$.

6. **B, C, and E** After distributing correctly and combining like terms, choices B, C, and E all become $12x + 10$.

7. **66** After dividing within the parentheses and multiplying out the exponent, you get $49 - 6 + 23$. There is now both addition and subtraction in the same problem. Solve the problem from left to right to get 66.

8. **438 – 227 = c; c = 211** You can write many different equations, but they must be equivalent to $438 - 227 = c$. The equation shown here uses subtraction to find the difference between the number of candies Anthony started with and how many his friends ate. Once you subtract, the result is 211 candies, which are the number of candies remaining.

9. **A, B, and C** Substituting 9 in for each variable makes the equations in choices A, B, and C true.

10.

Value of x	True	False
17		X
-5	X	
9	X	
11		X

Any numbers that are less than 10 make the inequality true. All numbers that are greater than 10 make the inequality false. So –5 and 9 are true, and 11 and 17 are false.

11. Part A. **d < 54**   The inequality $d < 54$ is correct because Joanna earns less than $54 per shift.

Part B.   **The number line should have an open circle at 54 with an arrow pointing to the left.**

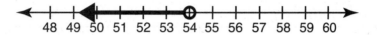

12. Part A.   **Packs of gum**   The independent variable is the number of packs of gum because that amount does not depend on the amount of money made by a sale.

Part B.   **Cost**   The dependent variable is the cost because that amount depends on how many packs of gum are purchased.

Part C.   **c = 1.25g**   This equation shows that you multiply the number of packs of gum by $1.25 to get the cost of those packs.

13. Part A.   **c = 85 + 50(t – 1)**   The plumber gets $85 just for the first hour. Any hours after that are charged at $50 per hour. So multiply 50 times the number of hours after the first hour, which is $t – 1$. Then add that to 85 to get the solution.

Part B.   **$210**   During the first hour, the cost is $85. Then subtract $3\frac{1}{2} – 1 = 2\frac{1}{2}$ to find the number of hours charged at $50 per hour. Multiply $2\frac{1}{2} \times 50$. The result is $125. Add the $125 to the $85 to get $210.

14. **22**   Once you plug in 9 for m you get $3(9) – 5$. First multiply 3×9. Then subtract $27 – 5$ to get 22.

15. **$38.95**   Multiply 70×0.20 to find the cost of the text messages. The cost equals $14.00. Then add $24.95 to $14.00 to get $38.95.

16. **C** 5^4 can be written as $5 \cdot 5 \cdot 5 \cdot 5$ because you multiply the base number, 5, by itself the number of times the exponent says to, which is 4.

17. **40n + 20j**   After you distribute the 5 groups of $8n$ and $4j$, you will have $40n + 20j$.

18. $\dfrac{35}{40}$ **or** $\dfrac{7}{8}$ To isolate the variable, n, multiply both sides by the reciprocal

of $\dfrac{4}{5}$. The reciprocal is $\dfrac{5}{4}$. Next, multiply $\dfrac{7}{10} \times \dfrac{5}{4} = \dfrac{35}{40}$ or $\dfrac{7}{8}$.

19. **10n + 15s**   To find the cost of the necklaces, multiply 10 times the number of necklaces, n. This results in 10n. To find the cost of the silver earrings, multiply 15 times the number of earrings bought, s. This results in 15s. Then simply add together 10n + 15s to find the total cost.

Chapter 4: Geometry

Practice Exercises—Areas of Polygons: Quadrilaterals and Triangles, pages 122–124

1. **32 square units**   Either count all the boxes or multiply the base (8 squares) by the height (4 squares).

2. **17.64 cm²**   Find the area of any quadrilateral by multiplying the base times the height. Since this is a square, you can multiply $s \times s$, where s equals the length of any side.

3. **49.5 in.²**   Find the area of a parallelogram by multiplying the base times the height. In this problem, the base is 9 inches and the height is 5.5 inches.

4. **124.065 cm²**   Find the area of a rectangle by multiplying the base times the height. In this problem, the base is 18.38 cm and the height is 6.75 cm.

5. **48 cm²**   Find the area of a triangle by using the formula $A = \dfrac{1}{2}(b \times h)$.
The base in the problem is 12 cm and the height is 8 cm. The **commutative property of multiplication** lets you multiply the numbers in any order. The easiest way to solve this problem is by taking $\dfrac{1}{2}$ of 12, which equals 6, and then multiplying that by 8: $6 \times 8 = 48$.

6. **29.4 cm²**   Use the formula $A = \dfrac{1}{2}(b \times h)$ to find the area of a triangle. The base is 9.8 and the height is 6. Take $\dfrac{1}{2}$ of 6, which equals 3. Then multiply that by 9.8: $3 \times 9.8 = 29.4$.

7. **6 cm²**   The formula to find the area of a triangle is $A = \dfrac{1}{2}(b \times h)$. The length of a diagonal is not in the formula. So the side that measures 5 cm is a distractor and is not used when finding the area of a triangle. To find the area, take $\dfrac{1}{2}$ of 4, which equals 2. Then multiply $2 \times 3 = 6$.

8. $65\frac{1}{4}$ **in.²** Use the formula $A = \frac{1}{2}(b \times h)$ to find the area of this triangle. The base is 14.5 and the height is 9. Take $\frac{1}{2}$ of 9, which equals 4.5. Then multiply $4.5 \times 14.5 = 65.25$.

Practice Exercises—Area of Irregular Polygons, pages 126–127

1. **140 cm²** Kite $ABCD$ is made of 4 triangles. One way to find the area of $ABCD$ is to find the area of two large triangles and then add them together. The top triangle measures 20 cm by 7 cm, and the bottom triangle also measures 20 cm by 7 cm. Use the area formula, $A = \frac{1}{2}(b \times h)$ for one of the triangles and then multiply the product by 2.

$$2\left(\frac{1}{2} \times 20 \times 7\right)$$

$$2(70)$$

$$140$$

   Alternatively, you could take the large bottom triangle (20 cm by 7 cm triangle) and translate it to the top. This would create one large parallelogram. The measurements for this parallelogram are 20 cm for the base and 7 cm for the height: $20 \times 7 = 140$.

2. **376 in.²** The top section of this shape is one large triangle of 24 by 8 inches. The bottom section is a trapezoid with two bases of 24 and 16 inches and a height of 14 inches. To find the area of the large triangle, multiply $\frac{1}{2}(24 \times 8) = 96$. To find the area of the trapezoid, use the formula $A = \frac{1}{2}(b_1 + b_2) \times h$. The top base is 24, and the bottom base is 16. Take $\frac{1}{2}$ of 40, which equals 20. Then multiply $20 \times 14 = 280$. Add the 280 and the 96 to get the total area.

3. **368.9 cm²** Find the area of this irregular shape by adding the area of the top triangle to the area of the bottom rectangle. The area of the triangle can be found by multiplying $23.8 \times \frac{1}{2} \times 9 = 107.1$. The area of the rectangle is found by multiplying the base 23.8 times the height 11. The area of the rectangle is 261.8. Add the two products together to get the total area of this polygon: $107.1 + 261.8 = 368.9$.

Practice Exercises—Surface Area, pages 133–135

1. **144 cm²** Find the surface area by adding the area of the square to the combined areas of the four triangles. The area of the square, or base, is found by multiplying one side by another side: $6 \times 6 = 36$. The area of one triangle is found by using the formula $A = \frac{1}{2}(b \times h)$. The base is 6 cm for each triangle, and the height is 9 cm: $\frac{1}{2}(6 \times 9) = 3 \times 9 = 27$. Multiply 27 by 4 because there are four triangular sides. Then add together the areas to find the surface area: $108 + 36 = 144$ square centimeters.

2. **108.4 cm²** To find the surface area of a rectangular prism, use the formula $2(l \times w) + 2(l \times h) + 2(w \times h)$. In this problem, the length and the width are 5 cm and 3.8 cm, respectively. The height is 4 cm. The top and the bottom are congruent, the two sides are congruent, and the front and the back are congruent. This illustrates the importance of multiplying each area by 2. Multiply the length by the width and then double.

$$5 \times 3.8 = 19$$
$$19 \times 2 = 38$$

Multiply the length by the height and then double.

$$5 \times 4 \text{ cm} = 20$$
$$20 \times 2 = 40$$

Multiply the width by the height and then double.

$$3.8 \times 4 = 15.2$$
$$15.2 \times 2 = 30.4$$

Now add together all of the areas to find the surface area.

$$38 + 40 + 30.4 = 108.4$$

3. **96 in.²** A cube has six congruent sides. The area of each side, or face, can be found by multiplying s^2: $4 \times 4 = 16$. Since there are 6 sides that each have an area of 16 square inches, multiply 16×6 to get the total surface area: $16 \times 6 = 96$ square inches.

4. **163.2 cm²** This triangular prism includes two congruent triangles and three congruent rectangles. The triangles each have a base of 6 and a height of 3.2. Each rectangle has a base or length of 6 and a height or width of 8. Use the formula $A = \frac{1}{2}(b \times h)$ to find the area of one of the triangles: $\frac{1}{2}(6 \times 3.2) = 3 \times 3.2 = 9.6$. Multiply $9.6 \times 2 = 19.2$ because there are two triangles that are the same size. Then multiply $8 \times 6 = 48$. Triple that amount because there are three rectangles of the same size: $48 \times 3 = 144$. Finally, add together all of the areas to find the surface area of the triangular prism: $144 + 19.2 = 163.2$.

5.

Statement	True	False
The surface area of box B is $1\frac{1}{2}$ times larger than the surface area of box A.		X
$2(24 \times 5) + 2(24 \times 8) + 2(5 \times 8)$ can be used to find the surface area of box A.	X	
The area of the base of box B is three times larger than the area of the base of box A.	X	

The first statement is false. The surface area of box A can be found by multiplying $2(24 \times 5) + 2(24 \times 8) + 2(5 \times 8) = 240 + 384 + 80 = 704$ in.². The surface area of box B can be found by multiplying

$$2(36 \times 10) + 2(36 \times 12) + 2(10 \times 12) = 720 + 864 + 240 = 1,824 \text{ in.}^2$$

Box B's surface area is more than double box A's.

The second statement is true. This equation is one way of finding the surface area of a rectangular prism. Find the area of the top and the bottom, add that to the area of the front and back, and then add that to the area of the two sides.

The third statement is true. The base of box A is $24 \times 5 = 120$. The base of box B is $36 \times 10 = 360$. Remember that 360 is three times as large as 120.

Practice Exercises—Volume, pages 138-139

1. **3.375 cm³** To find the volume of a cube, use the formula $V = s^3$. Since each side in a cube has the same measure and a cube is a rectangular prism, multiply the length by the width by the height: $1.5 \times 1.5 \times 1.5 = 3.375$.

2. **463.68 in.³** Find the volume of a rectangular prism by multiplying the length by the width by the height: $18.4 \times 4.2 \times 6 = 463.68$.

3. **78.75 cm³** To find the volume of a triangular prism, first find the area of the base. The base is a triangle, so use the formula $A = \frac{1}{2}(b \times h)$ to find its area: $\frac{1}{2}(3.5 \times 5) = 8.75$. Remember that when finding the volume of any figure, push the floor to the ceiling. This gives you the total space inside of a prism. Since the floor's area is 8.75, multiply 8.75×9 (the height, or length, of the prism) to get the total volume: $8.75 \times 9 = 78.75$.

4. Part A. **8 feet** The volume of a rectangular prism is found by multiplying the length by the width by the height. If you are given the volume and you need to find one of the other measures, start by multiplying the two given measures. Then divide that product into the total volume. In this problem, you are given a length of 18 and a width of 8: $18 \times 8 = 144$. Divide 1,152 by 144 to get the height of 8 feet.

   Part B. **96 boxes** First find the volume of each box. So use the volume formula for a rectangular prism: $3 \times 2 \times 2 = 12$ ft³. Then divide 12 into the total volume of 1,152 to get the total number of boxes that will fit inside of the storage room: $1,152 \div 12 = 96$.

5. **0.75 cm³** Use the formula $V = l \times w \times h$ to find the volume of a rectangular prism: $2 \times \frac{1}{2} \times \frac{3}{4} = \frac{3}{4} = 0.75$.

Practice Exercises—Polygons on the Coordinate Plane, pages 141–143

1. **30 square units** To find the area of a trapezoid, use the formula $A = \frac{1}{2}(b_1 + b_2) \times h$. The top base is the distance between point A (2, 6) and point B (5, 6). This distance is 3 units. The bottom base is the distance between point C (11, 1) and point D (2, 1). This distance is 9 units. The height is measured from point D (2, 1) straight up to point A (2, 6). The height is 5 units. Plug those values into the equation: $A = \frac{1}{2}(3 + 9) \times 5 = 6 \times 5 = 30$.

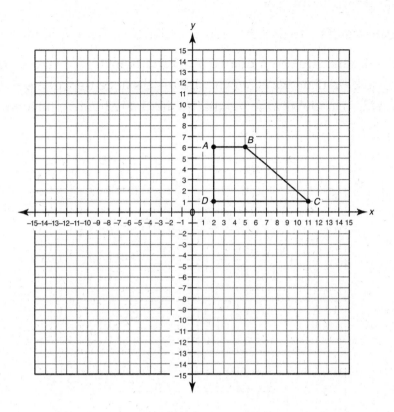

2. **45 square units** To find the area of a rectangle, use the formula $A = b \times h$.
   Use the distance between point D (2, –5) and point C (7, –5) to identify the
   base. The base distance is 5 units. Use the distance between point D (2, –5)
   and point A (2, 4). The height measurement is 9 units. The area is $9 \times 5 = 45$.

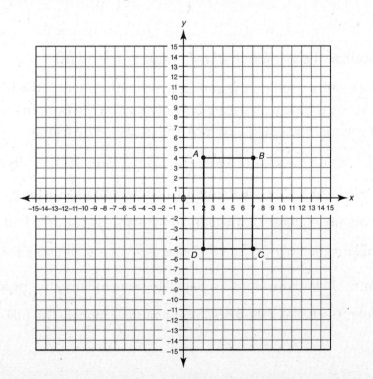

3. **12 square units** To find the area of a triangle use the formula $A = \frac{1}{2}(b \times h)$.

Use the distance between point B (2, 1) and point C (10, 1) to identify the base. The base distance is 8 units. Use the distance between point B (2, 1) and point A (2, 4) to identify the height. The height is 3 units. The area of the triangle is $A = \frac{1}{2}(8 \times 3) = 4 \times 3 = 12$.

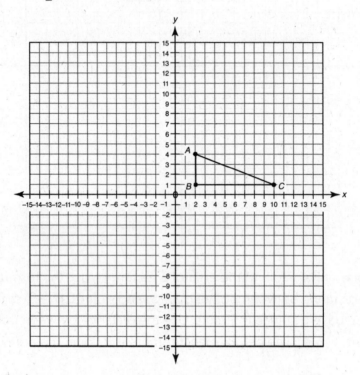

Practice Review Test—Geometry, pages 144–150

1. **32 square units** To find the area of a rectangle, multiply the base times the height. In this problem, there are 8 squares along the bottom and 4 squares in each column. You could also look at this as an 8 by 4 array.

2. **48 cm²** To find the area of a triangle use the formula $A = \frac{1}{2}(b \times h)$. Take $\frac{1}{2}$ of the $(b \times h)$, because a triangle is half the size of a rectangle, square, or parallelogram. All three of those quadrilaterals use $b \times h$ to find the area. In this problem, multiply $\frac{1}{2}(12 \times 8)$. Since $\frac{1}{2} \times 12 = 6$, multiply $6 \times 8 = 48$.

3. **$15\frac{5}{8}$ in.²** To find the area of a parallelogram, multiply the base times the height. The base of the parallelogram is $2\frac{1}{2}$ inches. The height of the

parallelogram is $6\frac{1}{4}$ inches, not $8\frac{2}{3}$ inches. The diagonal of any figure is not the height. The height is measured from any point on the base, straight up to the highest point of the shape. The value $3\frac{5}{6}$ inches is a distractor in this problem, because it does not represent any part of the actual base. To find the area, simply calculate $2\frac{1}{2} \times 6\frac{1}{4} = 15\frac{5}{8}$.

4. **Part A.** $\mathbf{18.5 \times h = 592}$ To find the area of a rectangle, multiply the base times the height. In this problem, the base is 18.5 and the area is 592. The height, h, is unknown.

   Part B. $\mathbf{h = 32\ centimeters}$ If you are given the base and the total area, divide the total area by the base to get the height: $592 \div 18.5 = h$. So $h = 32$.

5. **56 ft²** Use the formula $A = \frac{1}{2}(b_1 + b_2) \times h$ to find the area of a trapezoid. The two bases are the two sides that are parallel to each other. In this case, $b_1 = 16$ feet and $b_2 = 12$ feet. So $16 + 12 = 28$. Next, multiply $\frac{1}{2} \times 28 = 14$. Finally, multiply 14 by the height (4) to get the total area: $14 \times 4 = 56$.

6. **$42\frac{3}{4}$ in.²** To find the area of a rectangle, multiply the base by the height. In this problem, the base is $14\frac{1}{4}$ inches and the height is 3 inches.

7. **35 cm²** To find the area of a parallelogram, multiply the base by the height. In this problem, the base is 7 cm and the height is 5 cm. Remember that the height is always straight up and down. The diagonal (8) is not the height.

8. **3 inches** The volume of any rectangular prism can be found by using the formula $V = l \times w \times h$. In this problem, the length, the height, and the volume are given. You have to find the width. To find the width, first multiply the length times the height: $13 \times 9 = 117$. Then divide the total volume by 117, which gives $351 \div 117 = 3$.

9. **1,513 cm²** To find the surface area of any prism, find the area of all of the sides and add them together. In a rectangular prism, three of the sides have matching areas. Use the formula $2(l \times w) + 2(l \times h) + 2(w \times h)$ to find the total surface area.

   $$2(34 \times 8.5) + 2(34 \times 11) + 2(8.5 \times 11) = 578 + 748 + 187 = 1,513$$

10. **$21\frac{21}{32}$ in.²** To find the area of a triangle, use the formula $A = \frac{1}{2}(b \times h)$. We use this formula because a triangle is half the size of a rectangle,

parallelogram, or square. In this problem, multiply $\frac{1}{2} \times 10\frac{1}{2} \times 4\frac{1}{8}$. Since half of $10\frac{1}{2}$ is $5\frac{1}{4}$, you can find the area by multiplying $5\frac{1}{4} \times 4\frac{1}{8} = 21\frac{21}{32}$.

11. **10,500 ft²**   To find the surface area of a square pyramid, add the areas of the five sides together. Since the base is a square, find the area of the square by multiplying one side by another side: $50 \times 50 = 2,500$. The other four sides are triangles. Use the formula $A = \frac{1}{2}(b \times h)$ to find the area of each triangle: $\frac{1}{2} \times 50 \times 80 = 2,000$. You can either add all the sides together $(2,500 + 2,000 + 2,000 + 2,000 + 2,000 = 10,500)$ or you can add $2,500 + 4(2,000) = 2,500 + 8,000 = 10,500$.

12. **22,928.4 in.³**   To find the volume of a rectangular prism, find the area of the floor and multiply that number by the height of the prism. In this problem, the area of the floor of the file cabinet is already given. Multiply 424.6×54 to get the volume, which is 22,928.4.

13. Part A.   **6 feet**   The volume of a rectangular prism is found by multiplying $l \times w \times h$. In this problem, the length and the height are given. If you are missing one of the factors, divide the product of the other two factors. So $10 \times 7 = 70$. Then divide the entire volume by 70 to find the width: $420 \div 70 = 6$.

    Part B.   **30 boxes**   If the boxes can be stacked any way, find the volume of one box and divide that into the volume of the entire trailer. Find the volume of one box by multiplying $l \times w \times h$: $3 \times 2 \times 2\frac{1}{3} = 14$ ft³. Divide 420 by 14 to get the maximum number of boxes that can fit inside of the trailer: $420 \div 14 = 30$.

14. **42.875 cm³**   The volume of a cube can be found by using the formula $V = s^3$. Since each side in a cube is the same, multiply 3.5×3.5 first. This will give you the base area. Then multiply 12.25 by the height of the cube to find the volume: $12.25 \times 3.5 = 42.875$.

15. **48 square units**   Plot and label the four points: A (4, 3); B (4, 9); C (10, 9); D (14, 3). Connect A to B to C to D and then back to A. This creates a trapezoid on the grid. To find the area of a trapezoid, use the formula $A = \frac{1}{2}(b_1 + b_2) \times h$. The bottom base is 10 units, which is the distance from (4, 3) to (14, 3). The top base is 6 units, which is the distance from (4, 9) to

(10, 9). The height is 6 units. This is the straight up and down line from point *A* to point *B*. Use the following formula to calculate the area: $A = \frac{1}{2}(10 + 6) \times 6$ and $\frac{1}{2} \times 16 = 8$. So the area is $8 \times 6 = 48$.

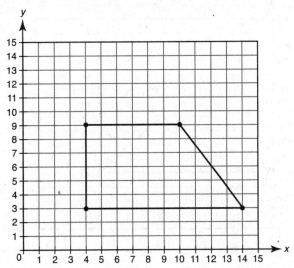

16. **Andy's candy box holds more candy. It has a volume of 40 cubic inches.** To find whose candy box holds more candy, find the volume of each box. This will give the amount of space inside of each box of candy. Volume is found by using the formula $V = l \times w \times h$. Tia's volume can be found by multiplying $4 \times 1\frac{1}{2} \times 6 = 36$ in.^{3}. Andy's volume can be found by multiplying $5 \times 2 \times 4 = 40$ in.^{3} Andy's candy box can hold more candy because his box has the greater volume.

17. **16.92 in.^{2}** Find the area of a triangle by using the formula $A = \frac{1}{2}(b \times h)$. In this problem, the base is 9.4 and the height is 3.6. So $\frac{1}{2} \times 9.4 = 4.7$ and $4.7 \times 3.6 = 16.92$.

18. **18 square units** Plot and label the three points: *H* (2, 4), *I* (7, 8), *J* (11, 4). Connect *H* to *I* to *J* and back to *H* again to form a triangle. To find the area of a triangle, use the formula $A = \frac{1}{2}(b \times h)$. The base of the triangle is the distance from points *H* to *J*. This distance can be found by counting units from *H* to *J*. The distance is 9 units. The height of the triangle can be found by using any point from the base and moving straight up to the highest point of the

triangle. Or, you can start at point *I* and draw a straight line down to the base. This is your height, which is 4 units. So $\frac{1}{2} \times 9 \times 4 = 4.5 \times 4 = 18$.

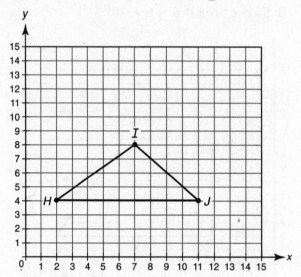

Chapter 5: Statistics

Practice Exercises—Statistical Questions, pages 152–153

1. **Not Statistical**   This is not a statistical question because there is only one answer: 60 minutes.

2. **Statistical**   This question is statistical because the heights of all the seventh graders will vary. There will be more than one measured height.

3. **Not Statistical**   This is not a statistical question because there is only one specific answer.

4. **Statistical**   This question is statistical because different students like different sports.

5.

Question	Yes	No
How much time do the students in my school spend watching television each night?	X	
How tall is Mount Everest?		X
How old are people when they start to drink coffee?	X	
How many students earned an A on the last test?		X
How many days are in a month?	X	

The first, third, and the fifth questions in the table are statistical because there is more than one solution to each question. How many students earned an A will give you one result, and Mount Everest has a specific height. This is why both of those questions are not statistical.

Practice Exercises—Measures of Central Tendency, pages 159–161

1. **Mean = 72**   The mean, or average, is found by adding all the numbers together. This total is 864. Then divide the sum of all the numbers by how many data points are in the set, which is 12. The mean is 864 ÷ 12 = 72.

   Median = 72   To find the median, or middle, line up all the numbers from least to greatest. Then eliminate numbers, one by one, from each side of the list. In this problem, two numbers will be left over: 70 and 74. Find the mean of those two numbers. Add 70 + 74 = 144 and divide 144 ÷ 2 = 72.

   Mode = 61   The mode is the number that occurs the most in the data set. In this set of data points, 61 is the only number that occurs twice. Therefore, 61 is the mode.

2. **98**   The mean is found by first adding all the numbers together. This total is 490. Then divide the sum by how many data points are in the set, which is 5. The mean is 490 ÷ 5 = 98.

3. **38 and 50**   The mode is the number that occurs more than any other number in the set of data points. In this set of data, both 38 and 50 occur more than the other numbers. They each occur three times.

4. **88**   When you are given the mean but a data point is missing, first multiply the mean by the total number of data points. In this problem, there are five data points including the missing value: 68 × 5 = 340. Next add the four data points: 124 + 36 + 52 + 40 = 252. Finally, subtract 252 from 340. This will give you the missing value: 340 – 252 = 88.

5. Part A.   **88**   To find the median, or middle, line up all of the numbers from least to greatest. Then eliminate numbers, one by one, from each side of the list. In this problem, there are an even amount of data points. Two numbers will be left over in the middle. The two numbers are 88 and 88. Their average is 88, so 88 is the median.

   Part B.   **79 and 88**   Both 79 and 88 occur twice in the data set. The other numbers only occur once.

Part C. **The mean would increase.** The mean is found by adding all the numbers together. The sum of the data points is 1,217. Divide the sum by the total number of data points, which is 14. So the mean is: 1,217 ÷ 14 = 86.9. Any time a new data point is added and that number is greater than the original average, the overall mean will increase.

Practice Exercises—Measures of Variation, page 166

1. Part A. **Upper quartile = 28; lower quartile = 20** To find the quartiles, first list the numbers from least to greatest.

~~19,~~ ~~20,~~ ~~20,~~ ~~22,~~ ~~24,~~ 27, ~~27,~~ ~~28,~~ ~~28,~~ ~~32,~~ ~~33~~
↑

Then find the median of the entire set by eliminating numbers, one by one, from each side. The median for all eleven numbers is 27. Next, find the middle of the numbers above 27, which are 27, 28, 28, 32, and 33. Again, eliminate numbers, one by one, from each side until you get to the median of the larger numbers. The upper quartile is 28.

19, 20, 20, 22, 24, 27, {27, 28, ⟨28⟩ 32, 33}

Follow the same steps for the lower quartile. The lower quartile is 20.

{19, 20, ⟨20⟩ 22, 24}, 27, 27, 28, 28, 32, 33

Part B. **8** To find the interquartile range, subtract the lower quartile from the upper quartile.

$$28 - 20 = 8$$

2. **3.25** To find the mean absolute deviation, first find the mean. To find the mean for this set of data, add all the numbers together (64) and then divide by how many data points you have (8). The mean is 8. Then find the absolute values of the differences between the mean and each data point.

$$|8 - 8| = 0$$
$$|8 - 10| = |-2| = 2$$
$$|8 - 7| = |1| = 1$$
$$|8 - 6| = |2| = 2$$
$$|8 - 13| = |-5| = 5$$
$$|8 - 5| = |3| = 3$$
$$|8 - 14| = |-6| = 6$$
$$|8 - 1| = |7| = 7$$

Find the mean, or average, of these eight numbers. First find the sum (26), and then divide by the number of data points (8).

$$26 \div 8 = 3.25$$

Practice Exercises—Box Plots and Other Data Displays, pages 172–174

1.

Statement	True	False
The median is 23.		X
The interquartile range is 4.	X	
The minimum is 8.	X	

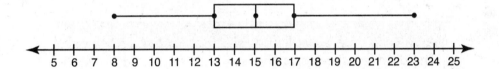

The first statement is false. The vertical line in the box portion of your box plot identifies the median. In the box plot above, the median line is at 15.

The second statement is true. The interquartile range is found by subtracting the lower quartile from the upper quartile: 17 – 13 = 4.

The third statement is true. The minimum is the first data point on the left in your box plot. The minimum is 8.

2.

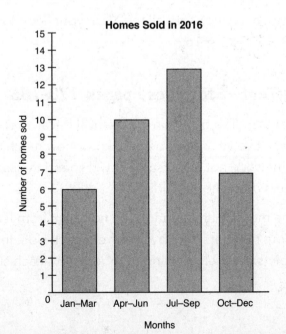

Part A. **23 homes were sold between April and September** To find this total add the two bars from Apr–Jun and Jul–Sep. 10 + 13 = 23.

Part B. **July to September had the most sales** The bar that measures the most sales is 13. This occurred between July and September.

Part C. **36 total homes sold** Add the four bars together. 6 + 10 + 13 + 7 = 36 total homes sold.

3. **18 puppies** To find the total number of data points in a line plot or dot plot, count all the X's or dots above the data points.

$$2 + 5 + 6 + 3 + 1 + 1 + 0 = 18$$

Data Descriptions—page 177

Statement	True	False
The data are skewed to the left.		X
The data are symmetrical.		X
Sandra surveyed sixteen friends.	X	

The first statement is false. The data points are skewed to the right because most of the data are on the left side of the line plot.

The second statement is false. The data are not symmetrical. Most of the data points are on the left side of the line plot.

The third statement is true. Add all the X's in your line plot above the data points: 3 + 4 + 7 + 1 + 1 = 16.

Practice Review Test—Statistics, pages 178–186

1. **Isabel is correct.** The question is statistical because there will be more than one answer. Even if Justin does not know how much time each student spends on homework, not every student will spend the same number of minutes or hours doing homework.

2. **26** To find the median, first arrange the numbers from least to greatest. Then start crossing out numbers, one by one, from each side. In this problem, there are six data points. After eliminating numbers from each side, two numbers

will remain (24 and 28). Find the middle of those two numbers by finding their average.

$$\frac{24+28}{2} = \frac{52}{2} = 26$$

3. Part A.   **82**   To find the mean, first add together all the numbers. Their sum is 820. Then divide by how many data points you have, which is 10. The mean is 820 ÷ 10 = 82.

    Part B.   **3.6**   To find the mean absolute deviation, find the absolute value difference between each data point and the mean.

$$|82 - 75| = |7| = 7$$
$$|82 - 85| = |{-3}| = 3$$
$$|82 - 88| = |{-6}| = 6$$
$$|82 - 89| = |{-7}| = 7$$
$$|82 - 83| = |{-1}| = 1$$
$$|82 - 77| = |5| = 5$$
$$|82 - 80| = |2| = 2$$
$$|82 - 81| = |1| = 1$$
$$|82 - 83| = |{-1}| = 1$$
$$|82 - 79| = |3| = 3$$

Then find the mean of those differences.

$$\frac{7+3+6+7+1+5+2+1+1+3}{10} = \frac{36}{10} = 3.6$$

4. **59**   An outlier is any number that is distinctly far away from all the other data points in your set. All the numbers in the data set are between 20 and 36 except for 59. Since 59 is not very close to the other numbers, it is an considered an outlier.

5. Part A.   **82**   Find the mean by first adding all the data points together. Then divide the sum by the number of data points: 1,230 ÷ 15 = 82.

    Part B.   **84**   To find the median, first organize the data points from least to greatest. Then cross out numbers, one by one, from each side until you get to the middle number, which is 84.

    Part C.   **27**   To find the range, subtract the minimum (66) from the maximum (93).

Part D. **Louie's thinking is incorrect.** The mode is the data point that occurs the most. There are three 90's in the data set. Since 90 occurs more than any other number, it is the mode.

6. Part A. **Mean** The mean, or average, is the best measure of center when all the numbers are fairly close to each other.

Part B. **Median** The median is the best measure of center when there is an outlier. All of the housing prices, except for one, are between 260 and 475. The outlier of 925 drastically changes the average (mean), but it minimally changes the median.

Part C. **Mode** The mode is the best measure of center when all the data points are fairly close to each other and there is one data point that occurs quite a few times more than any other data point. In this case, 16 occurs 4 times and all other points occur only once.

7. **B** Organize the numbers from least to greatest to find the minimum, maximum, median, lower quartile, and upper quartile.

27, 28, 28, 31, 32, 34, 35, 36, 37, 40, 40

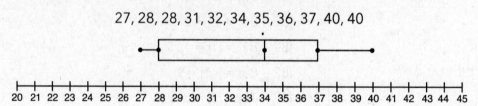

8.

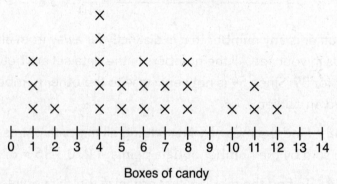

The median is 6. Find the median by crossing out **X**'s, one by one, from each side of the line plot.

The mode is 4. The mode is the number that occurs the most often. There are more 4's than any other number.

The range is 11. Subtract the minimum (1) from the maximum (12).

9. **Skewed left** A left skew occurs when most of the data points are on the right and there is a tail on the left. The tail represents few data points.

10.

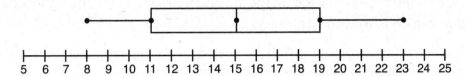

Statement	True	False
The median is 15.	X	
The upper quartile is 17.		X
The interquartile range is 8.	X	
The range is 19.		X

The first statement is true. The middle point in the box plot is 15. This is shown by the vertical line within the box.

The second statement is false. The upper quartile is the third quarter of the box plot. In this box plot the upper quartile is 19 and occurs at the right end of the box.

The third statement is true. The interquartile range (IQR) is the difference between the upper and lower quartiles: $19 - 11 = 8$.

The last statement is false. The range is 15. To find the range, subtract the minimum from the maximum: $23 - 8 = 15$.

11.

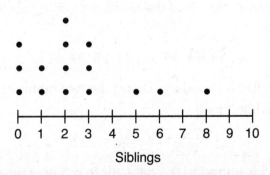

Siblings

Statement	True	False
The total number of friends surveyed is fifteen.	X	
The illustration is skewed to the left.		X
The dot plot shows a cluster of data from 0–3.	X	
The data are symmetrical.		X

The first statement is true. If you count all the dots, there are fifteen.

The second statement is false. The information is skewed to the right. When most of the data points are on the left and there is a tail to the right, a data distribution is skewed right.

The third statement is true. A large majority of numbers are listed from 0–3. This represents a cluster.

The last statement is false. The data are not symmetrical. When the data points are *not* skewed either right or left, they are said to be symmetrical.

12.

Statement	True	False
Adding the extra number will increase the mean.		X
Adding the extra number will increase the range.	X	
Adding the extra number will change the median.	X	

The first statement is false. The mean, or average, will not increase if you add a data point that is less than the original mean, such as 15. The original mean is 23.125.

The second statement is true. The range will increase. The range is found by subtracting the minimum from the maximum. In the original problem, the minimum is 18 and the maximum is 30. So the original range is 30 – 18 = 12. The new range will be computed by subtracting 15 from 30: 30 – 15 = 15.

The last statement is true. Find the median by lining up the numbers from least to greatest.

$$\text{18, 19, 19, 23, 24, 25, 27, 30}$$

The original median is found by adding the two numbers in the middle together and dividing by 2.

$$\frac{23+24}{2} = \frac{47}{2} = 23.5$$

If the number 15 is added to the data, there will now be an odd amount of data points.

$$\text{15, 18, 19, 19 (23) 24, 25, 27, 30}$$

The new median is 23.

13. **C** First list the numbers from least to greatest. Then cross out numbers, one by one, from each side until you get to the middle. The number 10 is the median because there are two 10's in the middle.

$$7, 8, 8, 9, 9, 9, 9, \boxed{10, 10}, 11, 12, 12, 13, 14, 15, 17$$

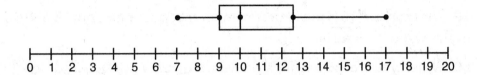

14. **3.75** Start by finding the mean. Add together all the numbers, and then divide the sum by the number of data points in the set.

$$74 + 76 + 84 + 81 + 79 + 83 + 87 + 76 = 640$$

$$\frac{640}{8} = 80$$

Then find out how far each number deviates from the mean.

$$|80 - 74| = |6| = 6$$
$$|80 - 76| = |4| = 4$$
$$|80 - 84| = |-4| = 4$$
$$|80 - 81| = |-1| = 1$$
$$|80 - 79| = |1| = 1$$
$$|80 - 83| = |-3| = 3$$
$$|80 - 87| = |-7| = 7$$
$$|80 - 76| = |4| = 4$$

Then find the mean of the absolute value differences.

$$\frac{6+4+4+1+2+3+7+4}{8} = \frac{30}{8} = 3.75$$

15. **98%** For Denali to earn a 90% average, or mean, she must have 450 total points accumulated.

$$\frac{450}{5} = 90$$

If Denali has an 88% average, she must have accumulated $88 \times 4 = 352$ points. Subtract the 352 points that Denali has already earned from the total points she needs to earn, which is 450.

$$450 - 352 = 98$$

Chapter 6: Math Practice Test 1

Computer Adaptive Test, pages 187–197

1. **44.367**   This is the solution after lining up the decimal points and subtracting.

2. **18**   The number 18 is the largest number that goes into both 18 and 36 evenly without a remainder.

3. **60**   When you are looking for a percent, the best way is to just divide. So divide 30 by 50. Since 30 is smaller than 50, add a decimal point to 30 and a few zeros after it. Always work out the quotient to two places after the decimal point. Then when changing a decimal to a percent, move the decimal point two places to the left.

4. $\frac{3}{8}$ When the first fraction is missing in a division of fractions problem, multiply the other two fractions together: $\frac{3}{4} \times \frac{1}{2} = \frac{3}{8}$. A way to check this is by multiplying across the top and across the bottom: $3 \times 1 = 3$ and $4 \times 2 = 8$.

5.

Statement	True	False
The number –2 is located to the left of –7 on the number line.		X
Both |–6| and –3 are located to the left of zero on the number line.		X
9 is located to the right of –3.5 on the number line.	X	

The first statement is false. The number –2 is located to the right of –7 on the number line because –2 is closer to 0.

The second statement is false. The number –3 is located to the left of 0 because it is a negative integer. However, \|–6\| = 6 and all positive integers are located to the right of the number 0.

The last statement is true. The number 9 is located to the right of –3.5 on the number line because 9 is positive. All positive integers are to the right of any negative rational numbers.

6. **7**   The complete equation is 48 + 56 = 8(6 + 7). After you distribute the 8 times both terms in the parentheses, the expression becomes 48 + 56.

7. **8 > –3**   This inequality shows that 8 is larger than –3.

8. **382**   In this order of operations problem, first subtract 14 from 17 since it is within the parentheses. The answer is 3. Then work out the exponential power of $5^3 = 5 \times 5 \times 5 = 125$. Next divide 7 into 49 to get 7. Your problem will now read $125 \cdot 3 + 7 = 382$.

9. **B, C, and E**   Choice A is incorrect because the simplified expression is equal to $8x + 48y$. Choice D is incorrect because the simplified expression is equal to $8x + 6y + 2$. Choices B, C, and E all simplify to $8x + 12y$.

10. Complete the table for the inequality $x > –4$.

Value of x	True	False	Reason
7	X		7 is greater than –4 because 7 is located to the right of –4 on the number line.
–4.8		X	–4.8 is located to the left of –4 on the number line because –4.8 is farther from 0 and to the left of 0.
0	X		0 is greater than –4 because 0 is located to the right of –4 on the number line.
1.55	X		1.55 is greater than –4 because 1.55 is located to the right of –4 on the number line.
–9		X	–9 is located to the left of –4 on the number line because –9 is farther from 0 and to the left of 0.

11.

Statement	True	False
The equation $t = 7 + w$ represents the relationship between the number of weeks and the total amount of money saved.		X
The total amount saved is 7 times the number of weeks.	X	
The amount of money that Daniel saves depends on the number of weeks.	X	

The first statement is false. The correct equation, based on information found in the table, is $t = 7w$. As the number of weeks increases, Daniel earns $7.00 more per week.

The second statement is true. The total amount saved is 7 times the number of weeks. Each week multiplied by 7 gives the total amount that Daniel saved.

The third statement is true. The amount that Daniel makes depends on how many weeks he saves. This is helpful when you are looking to identify independent and dependent variables. The money you make from working or the total amount you save depends on the number of hours you work or on how many weeks you save.

12. **D** How many students are in your math class is *not* a statistical question. If there is only one specific answer to the question, that question is not statistical.

13. **15 cm²** When finding the area of a triangle, use the formula $A = \frac{1}{2}(b \times h)$.

For this example, there are a few ways to find the total area. You multiply 5×6 and then divide by 2. Alternatively, you could take $\frac{1}{2}$ of 6, which equals 3, and then multiply that number by 5. Either way, the solution is 15 cm².

14. **12*n* = 48** You are only asked to write the equation from the words. When writing an equation, two expressions are equivalent. The first expression, "the product of twelve and a number" is located on the left side of the equals sign. The words "is equal to" represent the equals sign in this equation. The number 48 is the other expression and is located on the right side of the equals sign.

15. **60.52** The numerical product is already there. You must identify where the decimal point goes in the number 6,052. In both factors, 1.7 and 35.6, there are a total of two numbers after the decimal places combined. To place the decimal point correctly in a multiplication problem, move the decimal point to the left the total number of decimal places in the factor(s). Start moving it from the end of the number to the left. A great way to check your answer is by estimating $2 \times 35 = 70$. The only place you could put the decimal point into 6052 that would make it close to 70 is in between the 0 and the 5.

16. **A and E** The *x*- and *y*-coordinates of points in the third quadrant are both negative values. Point A and point E each have two negative values in each ordered pair.

17. **2.15** When setting up the problem, notice that both the divisor, 0.24, and the dividend, 0.516, have decimal points in them. You are finding how many groups of 0.24 go into 0.516. By estimating, you can see that there should be a little more than 2 groups because $0.24 \times 2 = 0.48$. Move the decimal points in both the dividend and the divisor two places to the right. The problem then reads 51.6 divided by 24. After moving the decimal point up to the quotient and adding a zero to the dividend, divide until the quotient terminates at 2.15.

18. **180** There are a few ways to solve this problem. You could write a proportion and solve for the number of widgets, w. $\dfrac{120 \text{ widgets}}{3 \text{ hours}} = \dfrac{w \text{ widgets}}{4.5 \text{ hours}}$ Then cross multiply: $3 \times w = 3w$ and $120 \times 4.5 = 540$. Divide 540 by 3 to get the solution: 180 widgets.

    Another method of solving this problem involves the use of a scale factor or multiplier. The multiplier from 3 hours to 4.5 hours is 1.5. If the hours increase by a multiplier of 1.5, the widgets increase by a multiplier of 1.5. $120 \times 1.5 = 180$.

19. **B** When finding a missing conversion factor, the units must cancel out. In the original rate of $\dfrac{6 \text{ yards}}{1}$, the numerator is represented by yards. The next factor must have yards as the denominator. This way, you can eliminate yards and find the unit you are looking for. The only factor where yards appears in the denominator is choice B. When you are all through converting, the only unit that should be left is the one that you are looking for. In this case, you were looking for inches.

$$\left(\frac{6 \text{ yards}}{1}\right) \times \left(\frac{3 \text{ feet}}{1 \text{ yard}}\right) \times \left(\frac{12 \text{ inches}}{1 \text{ foot}}\right) = x \text{ inches}$$

20. **39.1** An outlier is a number that does not represent the data set well. In this case, all the rational numbers in the data set, except for 39.1, are between 11 and 16. Since 39.1 is really far away from all of the other numbers, it drastically increases the mean of the data set and is therefore considered to be an outlier.

21. **30** The LCM can be found by listing the multiples of each number until you come to one that is common to both numbers.

6: 6, 12, 18, 24, 30

10: 10, 20, 30

22. **5 cm**   To find the area of a parallelogram, multiply the base times the height. In this problem, you are given the area and you must find the height of the parallelogram. Divide $42.5 \div 8.5 = 5$.

23. **12x + 27**   Distribute the 3 to both $4x$ and 9.

$$3 \times 4x = 12$$
$$3 \times 9 = 27$$

24. **20**   You need to find the total number of equal-sized sections on a page. A great strategy to use for this problem is a tape diagram. Identify that 60% on the tape diagram is equivalent to 12. Divide 12 by 6, which equals 2, because you are trying to find 10%. Once you know that 10% equals 2, 100% or the total equals 20.

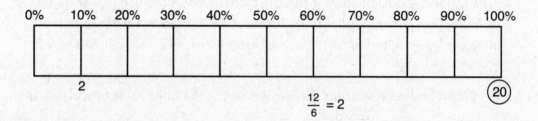

25. **17 bags**   There are a few ways to solve this problem. One way is to identify both numbers as monetary values: $4\frac{1}{4} = \$4.25$ and $\frac{1}{4} = \$0.25$. You can then realize that there are 17 quarters in $4.25. Alternatively, you can use division with mixed numbers.

$$4\frac{1}{4} \div \frac{1}{4} = 17$$

26. **1.5**   To find the MAD, first add all the numbers together and divide by how many numbers are in your data set. In this case, the numbers add up to 60. So $60 \div 12 = 5.5$ is the mean or average of your data set. To find the mean absolute deviation, calculate how far away from the mean each number is. Remember to use absolute value. For instance, 6 is 1 away from the mean, 9 is 4 away from the mean, 5 is 0 away from the mean, and 3 is 2 away from the mean. Continue this process until you have 12 new numbers and their distance from the mean. The absolute values of those distances are shown here.

$$1, 4, 0, 2, 1, 0, 1, 1, 2, 3, 0, 3$$

Add those 12 numbers together. The total is 18. Divide 18 by 12 to get the MAD of 1.5.

27. **C and D** In problem C, if you substitute 8 for *n*, the equation will read 8 + 9 = 17. Since both sides are equivalent, 8 makes the equation true. In problem D, if you substitute 8 for *n*, the equation is 8 • 5 = 40. Since both sides are equivalent, 8 makes the equation true.

28. **The 5-bar package of soap is the better deal.** To find the better price, find the unit price of each item and compare. To find the unit price, divide the dollar amount by the number of items.

$$\$2.89 \div 3 = \$0.96$$

The cost of each bar of soap in the 3-pack is $0.96.

$$\$4.75 \div 5 = \$0.95$$

The cost of each bar of soap in the 5-pack is $0.95.

29. Part A.

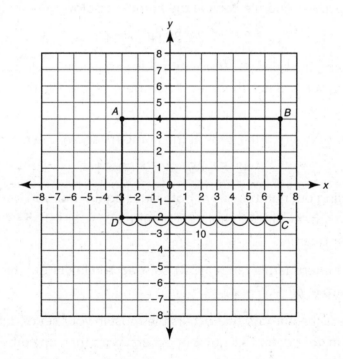

Part B. **10** The distance between two points can be found using different methods. One way is by creating an absolute value expression and solving it. Points *C* and *D* each have the same *y*-value. You do not need that value to find the distance. One *x*-value is 7, and the other *x*-value is –3. Both points are in different quadrants. Point *C* is in Quadrant IV, and point *D* is in Quadrant III. When the points are in different quadrants add their absolute values.

$$|7| + |-3| = 7 + 3 = 10$$

30.

Median	48
Lower Quartile	39
Upper Quartile	67
Interquartile Range	28
Mode	48

To find the median, list the numbers from smallest to greatest.

23, 29, 33, 39, 40, 44, 48, 48, 48, 57, 65, 67, 72, 80, 91

Start crossing out numbers from each side of your list until there is just one number left. That number is the number in the middle or the median. Since there are 15 numbers in your list, the 8th number is your median.

To find the lower quartile, look at the numbers below the median in your list.

23, 29, 33, 39, 40, 44, 48

Start crossing out numbers from both sides again until you get to the middle of these numbers. Since there are 7 numbers in your list, the 4th number is your lower quartile.

To find the upper quartile, look at the numbers above the median in your list.

48, 57, 65, 67, 72, 80, 91

Start crossing out numbers from both sides again until you get to the middle of these numbers. Since there are 7 numbers in your list, the 4th number is your upper quartile.

To find the interquartile range (IQR), subtract the lower quartile from the upper quartile: $67 - 39 = 28$.

The mode is the number that occurs the most in your set of data. There are three 48s in your data. This number occurs more than any other number. So 48 is the mode.

31. **Ivan is correct.** Lonnie multiplied $3 \times 3 \times 3$ and then combined the product of 27 with the two variables x and y. Ivan multiplied the 3 that is outside of the parentheses by both terms inside the parentheses: $3 \times 3x = 9x$ and $3 \times 3y = 9y$.

32. **1,803R15**   24 goes into 43,287 a total of 1,803 times with a remainder of 15. Make sure you check your solution by multiplying back. Multiply 1,803 times 24. The product is 43,272. Then add 15 to that total. Since the result equals 43,287, you have the correct quotient.

33. **B and D**   Choice B shows when a base number of 6 is expanded correctly: $6^2 = 6 \cdot 6$. Choice D shows when an expanded form is turned into an exponential power: $6 \cdot 6 \cdot 6 \cdot 6 = 6^4$.

34. **2,040 square inches**   To find the volume of a rectangular prism, use the formula $l \times w \times h$. The length and the width make up the area of the base of the prism. Multiply the base area by the height of the prism to find the total volume.

35.

Statement	True	False
9 students scored 80 on their quiz.	X	
The mean score is 80.		X
More than half of the class scored 90 or 100.	X	

The first statement is true. 9 of the students scored an 80 on the quiz because there are 9 dots at 80 on the dot plot.

The second statement is false. The mean in the problem is 87. First, add all the numbers together: $9 \times 80 = 720$; $8 \times 90 = 720$; $3 \times 100 = 300$; $300 + 720 + 720 = 1,740$. Divide 1,740 by the total number of dots, 20. The mean is 87.

The last statement is true. There are 11 students who scored 90 or 100. There are 9 students who scored 80. This is represented by the number of dots on top of each score.

Performance Task, pages 198–199

1. **9.5 feet**   To find the volume of a rectangular prism, multiply the base area by the height. In this case, the base area and the volume are given. To find the height, divide the total volume by the base area: $456 \div 48 = 9.5$.

2. **22**   To find the median, first list the numbers from least to greatest.

$$5, \cancel{10}, \cancel{15}, \cancel{18}, \cancel{19}, \cancel{20}, \cancel{22}, 22, 22, \cancel{24}, \cancel{25}, \cancel{27}, \cancel{29}, \cancel{30}, \cancel{60}, \cancel{65}$$

Then eliminate numbers, one by one, from each side until you get to the middle. In this problem, there are two numbers in the middle. Both numbers are 22.

3. **The mean would decrease.**   The mean is the average. It is found by adding all the data points together and dividing by how many numbers you have. If you eliminate any data points that are above the mean, the average will decrease.

4. Part A.   **4(28) + 2(37)**   The expression represents four groups of $28 because there are four children. The expression also shows two groups of $37 because there are two adults. The total cost is the combination of these two terms.

   Part B.   **$186**   First multiply: $4 \times 28 = 112$ and $2 \times 37 = 74$. Then add: $112 + 74 = \$186$.

5. **$c \geq 40$**   This inequality represents the fact that children must be at least 40 inches or taller to ride the roller coaster.

6. **$8.20**   Use the expression 4(7.95) to find the total cost of the four value meals, which is $31.80. Then subtract 31.80 from 40 to find the change Ricky's parents receive: $40.00 - 31.80 = 8.20$.

Chapter 7: Math Practice Test 2

Computer Adaptive Test, pages 201–214

1. **35.814**   After multiplying $381 \times 94 = 35,814$, you need to identify where the decimal point should go in your product. One way to place the decimal point is by estimating the two factors. Since 3.81 is close to 4 and 9.4 is close to 9, multiply $4 \times 9 = 36$. If you know that your product is close to 36, the only place you could put the decimal point is between the 5 and the 8. You could also add decimal places in the factors and then using that sum to place the decimal point in the product. There are two decimal places in 3.81. There is one decimal place in 9.4. Add the decimal places. Start from the right end of 35,814. Move your decimal point three places to the left to form 35.814.

2.   Find the missing value in the ratio table:

x	y
3	24
4	32
7	**56**
9	72

The number 56 is the missing y-value. The multiplier from each x-value to each y-value is 8 since $3 \times 8 = 24$, $4 \times 8 = 32$, and $9 \times 8 = 72$. So $7 \times 8 = 56$.

3.   **October 23**   The least common multiple (LCM) of 5 and 4 is 20. This can be found by creating lists of multiples for each number. If Tina played both sports on October 3 and the LCM is 20, she will perform both activities again 20 days later.

$$4: 4, 8, 12, 16, \widehat{20}$$

$$5: 5, 10, 15, \widehat{20}$$

4.   **5**   There are many ways to find the GCF of 2 different numbers. One way is to create tables of factors for both numbers.

25	
1	25
⑤	5

55	
1	55
⑤	11

5.   **7**   To find the distance between two points, count the number of units from one point to another. Point B (2, −3) lies in Quadrant IV. Point C (2, 4) lies in Quadrant I. Start at either point, and count from one to the other. Some students make the mistake of counting one of the starting points as the number 1. Do not do this. A way to check your answer is by looking at the y-values in both ordered pairs: $3 + 4 = 7$ and $4 − 3 = 1$. The only possible

answers you could get are 1 and 7. Since you are traveling from one quadrant to another, add the absolute values to get 7.

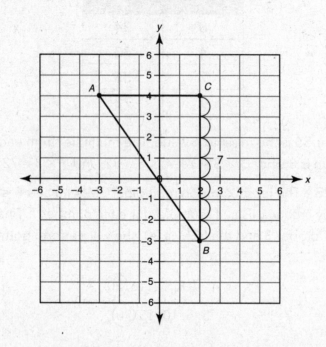

6. **A and D** Choice A is correct because two terms are multiplied by 3^4 via the distributive property. Remember that terms are separated by a plus (+) or a minus (−) sign. Choice D is correct because the term $4n$ has a coefficient of 4. A coefficient is the number in front of a variable.

7. $\frac{1}{3}$ When the second fraction in a division of fraction problem is missing, divide the first fraction by the third fraction to get the divisor. To check the answer, plug in $\frac{1}{3}$ into the problem.

$$\frac{3}{10} \div \frac{1}{3} = \frac{3}{10} \times \frac{3}{1} = \frac{9}{10}$$

8. **200** Use either an equation or a tape diagram to find the solution. First change the percent into a fraction in lowest terms.

$$20\% = \frac{20}{100} \div \frac{20}{20} = \frac{1}{5}$$

Then set up the equation $\frac{1}{5}n = 40$. Multiply both sides by the reciprocal of $\frac{1}{5}$.

$$\frac{5}{1} \times \frac{1}{5}n = \frac{40}{1} \times \frac{5}{1}$$

Remember that whatever you do to one side of the equation you must do to the other side of the equation. On the left side, the result is 1*n*, which is *n*. On the right side, you are left with 200.

9. **45 words in 1 minute**   To find the unit rate, divide both numbers in your rate by the denominator.

$$\frac{135\,\text{words}}{3\,\text{minutes}} \div \frac{3}{3} = \frac{45\,\text{words}}{1\,\text{minute}}$$

10. **A and C**   Choice A shows the correct way of changing a percent to a fraction: $65\% = \frac{65}{100}$. Choice C shows the correct way of changing a percent to a decimal: $65\% = 0.65$. To change a percent to a decimal, move the decimal point two places to the left. If the original percent does not have a decimal point in the number, add one at the end of the number. The Smarter Balanced Assessment might try to trick you by putting in an expression like 6.5×30. This would also be correct because 0.65 of 300 = 195 and $6.5 \times 30 = 195$.

11. Part A.   **c + 62 = 107**   Louie started with some playing cards. If the amount is not given, assign it a variable. In the problem, the assigned variable is *c*. He traded for or received 62 more cards. He now has a total of 107 cards.

    Part B.   **c = 45**   Subtract 62 from both sides of the equation to isolate the variable: $c + 62 - 62 = 107 - 62$. The left side includes numbers that can be crossed out. The variable, *c*, is now isolated to equal whatever is left on the right side: $c = 45$.

12. Consider the following set of numbers (18,15,17,19,18,18,20,14,23,18).

Statement	True	False
The mode of the data is 23.		X
The median of the data is 18.	X	
The mean of the data is 18.	X	
If another 18 was added to the data set, the mean would increase.		X

The first statement is false. The mode is not 23. The mode is the number that occurs the most in your data set. Since there are four 18s in the data set, 18 is the mode.

The second statement is true. To find the median, place the numbers in order from least to greatest.

$$14, 15, 17, 18, 18, 18, 18, 19, 20, 23$$

Start crossing off numbers, one from each side, until you get to the middle. In this case, there are two numbers left in the middle. Since both of those numbers are the same, 18, that is your median.

The third statement is true. The mean for the data set is 18. Add all the numbers together. Then divide by how many numbers are in your data set: $180 \div 10 = 18$.

The last statement is false. If another 18 was added to the data set, the mean would stay the same. If a number greater than 18 was added to the data set, the mean would increase.

13. **$5h + 7$**   To combine variable terms, the variable must be the same. There are three variable terms that all have the same letter, h. Add the coefficients in front of the three h terms: $2 + 1 + 2 = 5$. Then add the numerical terms: $3 + 4 = 7$.

14. **6,118 cm³**   To find the volume of a rectangular prism, multiply the base area by the height of the prism. The base area is found by multiplying the length by the width: $23 \times 19 = 437$. Then multiply that by the height of the prism: $437 \times 14 = 6{,}118$. Remember to cube the unit because you are finding three-dimensional cubes that stack up to fill the air space inside of the prism.

15.

Number of Boxes Sold, n	Amount of Money Collected in Dollars, d
1	25
2	50
3	75
4	100
8	200

Part A.   **$n = 2$; $d = 25$; $d = 200$**   To find the missing values for d, look at the two lines that are complete. When you look at the third and fourth rows, you can see that the multiplier between boxes sold and money collected is 25. To find the missing value for n, use $50 \div 25 = 2$.

Part B. **25n = d** Multiply the number of boxes by 25 to reach the amount of money collected. When writing an equation, remember that both variables will be present. You need to figure out which variable is multiplied by the unit rate to equal the other variable. One way to check this is by plugging in a value for one of the variables. If it checks out, then you have written the correct equation.

16. **Anissa had the smaller absolute deviation from the mean.** To find the deviation from the mean, subtract the scores from the mean. The average was 82%. Anissa's score was 4 points away from the mean: $82 - 78 = 4$. Theodore's score was 9 points away from the mean: $91 - 82 = 9$.

17. **1,212.75 ft²** To find the area of a triangle, use the formula $A = \frac{1}{2}(b \times h)$. In this problem, it is easier to take $\frac{1}{2}$ of 42 first. Then multiply $21 \times 57.75 = 1{,}212.75$. Remember that the unit is written in square feet because you are representing a two-dimensional figure.

18. **D** Remember to Keep, Change, and Flip when dividing fractions by other fractions. The first fraction $\frac{3}{4}$ stays the same. The division sign turns into a multiplication sign. Then flip the second fraction over to form the reciprocal.

19. **−95** Integers are positive or negative whole numbers, including zero. In this case, the submarine dove below the surface of the water. The surface of the water represents 0 on the number line. Any values below 0 on the number line are represented with a negative sign in front of the number.

20. **B** The values listed are represented only on number line B.
$$-3, -1\frac{1}{2}, \frac{1}{4}, 1\frac{3}{4}, 2$$

21. **B and D** In this expression, you can combine the four v values. The coefficient in front of each v is 1. Therefore, you have $4 + 4v$. Choice B is correct because it uses the commutative property of addition: $4v + 4 = 4 + 4v$. Choice D is correct because it uses the distributive property correctly. When distributing a number outside of the parentheses, you must multiply that value times both terms inside of the parentheses: $4(1 + v) = 4 + 4v$. Again, this expression is equivalent because you can switch the order of multiplication or addition and not change the value in the problem.

22. **127.5 cm²** Plug the values into the formula $A = \frac{1}{2}(b_1 + b_2) \times h$: $A = \frac{1}{2}(10 + 5) \times 17$. This is equivalent to $7.5 \times 17 = 127.5$. Remember that

the unit is written in square centimeters because you are representing a two-dimensional figure.

23. **42**   First add the two numbers inside the parentheses. Then solve the problem from left to right. When there are multiplication or division signs in the same problem, solve them from left to right. It doesn't matter which one is written first; just work the equation from left to right.

$$108 \div (13 + 5) \times 7$$

$$108 \div 18 \times 7$$

$$6 \times 7$$

$$42$$

24.

x	y
2	9
4	18
10	**45**
12	54

45   To find the missing value, look at the lines that include both an x- and a y-value. When looking at lines 1, 2, and 4, you can determine the multiplier by dividing the smaller number by the larger number: $9 \div 2 = 4.5$ and $54 \div 12 = 4.5$. The multiplier in the problem is 4.5 or $4\frac{1}{2}$. To find the missing value, multiply $10 \times 4.5 = 45$.

25.

Statement	True	False
The distance from between –17 and 0 is the same as between |–17| and 0 on the number line.	X	
On a number line, |7| and –7 are the same point.		X
The distance between –8 and 0 on the number line is |8| units.	X	

The first statement is true. $|{-17}| = 17$ since –17 and 17 are both the same distance from 0.

The second statement is false. The absolute value of 7 = 7. On a number line, 7 and −7 are not the same point on a number line.

The third statement is true. The distance between −8 and 0 on the number line is 8 units. Since the absolute value of 8 = 8 and distance is always positive, the statement is correct.

26. **4** To understand which operation to use, you must look at the key word "cut." Maddox is taking an original piece of wood and cutting it into smaller pieces. First change the mixed numbers into improper fractions.

$$4\frac{2}{3} \div 1\frac{1}{6} = \frac{14}{3} \div \frac{7}{6}$$

Then Keep, Change, and Flip to solve the problem.

$$\frac{14}{3} \times \frac{6}{7} = \frac{84}{21} = 4$$

27. **The correct place for |-1.8| is between 1 and 2.** The absolute value of any number is positive; 1.8 is between 1 and 2. Since there are ten lines between each integer, every line stands for tenths. So 1.8 is placed on the eighth line after positive 1.

The correct place for −(−2.5) is between 2 and 3. This is an example of using the distributive property correctly. The number on the outside of the parentheses is −1. In seventh grade, you will learn that multiplying a negative number by another negative number yields a positive answer. You could also think of this as taking the opposite of −2.5.

The correct place for −0.7 is between 0 and −1. Start at 0 and move seven lines to the left. The dot should be placed at three-tenths or three lines to the right of −1.

28. **z = 12** Solve this problem by dividing both sides by 9.

$$\frac{9z}{9} = \frac{108}{9}$$

$$z = 12$$

29. Part A. **4c = 24** This is a multiplication equation because you need to take the number of chores times the amount of money Matthew makes per chore. This total will come out to $24.

Part B. **c = 6** Solve this problem by dividing both sides by 4.

$$\frac{4c}{4} = \frac{24}{4}$$

$$c = 6$$

30. **C** A box plot is created from a 5-number summary: the maximum, the minimum, the lower and upper quartiles, and the median. First list the numbers from least to greatest.

$$2, 3, 3, 5, 7, 8, 8, 9, 11$$

Be sure to check that you haven't forgotten any of the numbers. Once they are in order from least to greatest, the maximum is on the far right (11), and the minimum is on the far left (2). To find the median, start crossing out numbers from both sides of your list until you get to the middle. Since there are nine numbers in your set, the fifth number is your median, 7. To find the lower quartile, cross out numbers from both sides of the numbers below 7. Since there are four numbers, you will be left with two numbers in the middle of your lower set. Both are 3, so that is your lower quartile. There are also four numbers that are above the median, 7. Cross out until you get to the middle two numbers. One of the numbers is 8, and one of the numbers is 9. The upper quartile is the number between 8 and 9: 8.5. Choice C is the only box plot that displays this 5-number summary correctly.

31. **47R13** The quotient after dividing 39 into 1,846 is 47R13. To check your answer, multiply $47 \times 39 = 1,833$. Then add the remainder: $1,833 + 13 = 1,846$.

32. **5 miles** To find the distance between two points, first plot both points on a coordinate plane. Then count from one point to the other. Remember, do not start counting from the starting point.

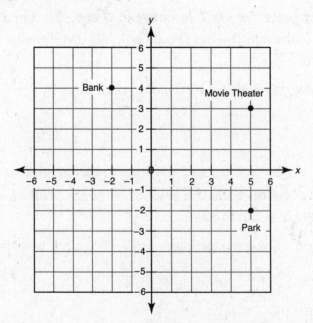

33. **42.75 in.²**   This problem wants you to find the total surface area of a rectangular prism. There are six sides to the rectangular prism. The top and the bottom have the same area. The front and back have the same area. The two sides have the same area. Use the expression

$$2(3 \times 1.5) + 2(3 \times 3.75) + 2(1.5 \times 3.75)$$

to find the total surface area of the cereal box. After multiplying the three sets of parentheses, the solution is 9.00 + 22.50 + 11.25 = 42.75.

34. **66**   To solve this expression, first plug in 3 for y. Remember that when you plug in a number for a variable and it is next to another number, you must multiply the two numbers. So $12y$ means that you have 12 groups of whatever y happens to be. After multiplying 12×3, you will then multiply 5×6 next because multiplication comes before addition: 36 + 30 = 66.

35. **C**   The inequality shows that all numbers greater than $-1\frac{1}{2}$ make the inequality true. An open circle should be placed at $-1\frac{1}{2}$. An open circle shows that all the values for m are greater than $-1\frac{1}{2}$ but not equal to it. All positive values make this inequality true. Draw the arrow to the right to indicate all the values that make this inequality true.

Performance Task, pages 215–218

1.

Number of Square Feet	Cost
10	$38
20	$76
40	**$152**
60	$228
100	$380

The multiplier from the left column to the right column is 3.8 or 3.80. So the missing value is $40 \times 3.8 = 152$.

2. **$658.00**   To find the total cost of the floor, multiply the cost per square foot of the ceramic tile by the number of square feet in the room: $140 \times 4.70 = 658.00$.

3. **The expression is incorrect.** If three of the rooms have wool carpeting installed and five of the rooms have porcelain tile installed, the correct expression is $3w + 5p$. Multiply the number of rooms by the style of flooring. The expression Mrs. Nunez wrote includes multiplying the style of flooring by itself three or five times, which is incorrect.

4. Part A. $c \leq \$12,000$ When a word problem includes the words "at most," it refers to the maximum number allowed. In this problem, $12,000 is the most the family can spend. The Nunez family can spend the exact amount $12,000 or less.

   Part B. **A closed circle will be drawn at 12,000 with an arrow pointing to the left.**

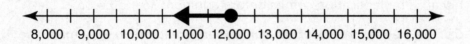

8,000	9,000	10,000	11,000	12,000	13,000	14,000	15,000	16,000

5. Part A. **180 square feet** Let b_1 equal 10 feet, b_2 equal 20 feet, and h equal 12 feet. Then plug the numbers into the equation to find the number of square feet of the trapezoid-shaped room.

$$A = \frac{1}{2}(b_1 + b_2) \times h$$

$$A = \frac{1}{2}(10 + 20) \times 12$$

$$A = \frac{1}{2}(30) \times 12$$

$$A = 15 \times 12$$

$$A = 180$$

   Part B. **$783.00** Multiply the area of the room by the cost per square feet of marble, which is $4.35.

$$180 \times 4.35 = 783$$

6. Part A. **4** To find the median, first arrange the data points from least to greatest. Then start crossing off numbers, one by one, so that only one number remains.

$$2, 3, 3, 4, 4, 4, 5, 5, 6$$

Part B. **4** To find the mean, add all the numbers together. Then divide the sum by the total number of data points.

$$\frac{2+3+3+4+4+4+5+5+6}{9} = \frac{36}{9} = 4$$

Part C. **Mr. Nunez is incorrect.** The mode is the number that occurs the most often in a data set. Mr. Nunez might have been thinking of the maximum, which is the largest value in the data set. In this problem, 4 is the mode because it occurs more than the other data points.

Common Core and Mathematical Practice Standards

APPENDIX A

Grade 6 Common Core Math Standards

Understand ratio concepts and use ratio reasoning to solve problems.

CCSS.Math.Content.6.RP.A.1 Understand the concept of a ratio and use ratio language to describe a ratio relationship between two quantities. *For example, "The ratio of wings to beaks in the bird house at the zoo was 2:1, because for every 2 wings there was 1 beak." "For every vote candidate A received, candidate C received nearly three votes."*

CCSS.Math.Content.6.RP.A.2 Understand the concept of a unit rate a/b associated with a ratio a:b with b ≠ 0, and use rate language in the context of a ratio relationship. *For example, "This recipe has a ratio of 3 cups of flour to 4 cups of sugar, so there is 3/4 cup of flour for each cup of sugar." "We paid $75 for 15 hamburgers, which is a rate of $5 per hamburger."*

CCSS.Math.Content.6.RP.A.3 Use ratio and rate reasoning to solve real-world and mathematical problems, e.g., by reasoning about tables of equivalent ratios, tape diagrams, double number line diagrams, or equations.

CCSS.Math.Content.6.RP.A.3.A Make tables of equivalent ratios relating quantities with whole-number measurements, find missing values in the tables, and plot the pairs of values on the coordinate plane. Use tables to compare ratios.

CCSS.Math.Content.6.RP.A.3.B Solve unit rate problems including those involving unit pricing and constant speed. *For example, if it took 7 hours to mow 4 lawns, then at that rate, how many lawns could be mowed in 35 hours? At what rate were lawns being mowed?*

CCSS.Math.Content.6.RP.A.3.C Find a percent of a quantity as a rate per 100 (e.g., 30% of a quantity means 30/100 times the quantity); solve problems involving finding the whole, given a part and the percent.

CCSS.Math.Content.6.RP.A.3.D Use ratio reasoning to convert measurement units; manipulate and transform units appropriately when multiplying or dividing quantities.

Apply and extend previous understandings of multiplication and division to divide fractions by fractions.

CCSS.Math.Content.6.NS.A.1 Interpret and compute quotients of fractions, and solve word problems involving division of fractions by fractions, e.g., by using visual fraction models and equations to represent the problem. *For example, create a story context for (2/3) ÷ (3/4) and use a visual fraction model to show the quotient; use the relationship between multiplication and division to explain that (2/3) ÷ (3/4) = 8/9 because 3/4 of 8/9 is 2/3. (In general, (a/b) ÷ (c/d) = ad/bc.) How much chocolate will each person get if 3 people share 1/2 lb. of chocolate equally? How many 3/4-cup servings are in 2/3 of a cup of yogurt? How wide is a rectangular strip of land with length 3/4 mi and area 1/2 square mi?*

Compute fluently with multi-digit numbers and find common factors and multiples.

CCSS.Math.Content.6.NS.B.2 Fluently divide multi-digit numbers using the standard algorithm.

CCSS.Math.Content.6.NS.B.3 Fluently add, subtract, multiply, and divide multi-digit decimals using the standard algorithm for each operation.

CCSS.Math.Content.6.NS.B.4 Find the greatest common factor of two whole numbers less than or equal to 100 and the least common multiple of two whole numbers less than or equal to 12. Use the distributive property to express a sum of two whole numbers 1–100 with a common factor as a multiple of a sum of two whole numbers with no common factor. *For example, express 36 + 8 as 4(9 + 2).*

Apply and extend previous understandings of numbers to the system of rational numbers.

CCSS.Math.Content.6.NS.C.5 Understand that positive and negative numbers are used together to describe quantities having opposite directions or values (e.g., temperature above/below zero, elevation above/below sea level, credits/debits, positive/negative electric charge); use positive and negative numbers to represent quantities in real-world contexts, explaining the meaning of 0 in each situation.

CCSS.Math.Content.6.NS.C.6 Understand a rational number as a point on the number line. Extend number line diagrams and coordinate axes familiar from previous grades to represent points on the line and in the plane with negative number coordinates.

CCSS.Math.Content.6.NS.C.6.A Recognize opposite signs of numbers as indicating locations on opposite sides of 0 on the number line; recognize that the opposite of the opposite of a number is the number itself, e.g., −(−3) = 3, and that 0 is its own opposite.

CCSS.Math.Content.6.NS.C.6.B Understand signs of numbers in ordered pairs as indicating locations in quadrants of the coordinate plane; recognize that when two ordered pairs differ only by signs, the locations of the points are related by reflections across one or both axes.

CCSS.Math.Content.6.NS.C.6.C Find and position integers and other rational numbers on a horizontal or vertical number line diagram; find and position pairs of integers and other rational numbers on a coordinate plane.

CCSS.Math.Content.6.NS.C.7 Understand ordering and absolute value of rational numbers.

CCSS.Math.Content.6.NS.C.7.A Interpret statements of inequality as statements about the relative position of two numbers on a number line diagram. *For example, interpret –3 > –7 as a statement that –3 is located to the right of –7 on a number line oriented from left to right.*

CCSS.Math.Content.6.NS.C.7.B Write, interpret, and explain statements of order for rational numbers in real-world contexts. *For example, write –3°C > –7°C to express the fact that –3°C is warmer than –7°C.*

CCSS.Math.Content.6.NS.C.7.C Understand the absolute value of a rational number as its distance from 0 on the number line; interpret absolute value as magnitude for a positive or negative quantity in a real-world situation. *For example, for an account balance of –30 dollars, write |-30| = 30 to describe the size of the debt in dollars.*

CCSS.Math.Content.6.NS.C.7.D Distinguish comparisons of absolute value from statements about order. *For example, recognize that an account balance less than –30 dollars represents a debt greater than 30 dollars.*

CCSS.Math.Content.6.NS.C.8 Solve real-world and mathematical problems by graphing points in all four quadrants of the coordinate plane. Include use of coordinates and absolute value to find distances between points with the same first coordinate or the same second coordinate.

Apply and extend previous understandings of arithmetic to algebraic expressions.
CCSS.Math.Content.6.EE.A.1 Write and evaluate numerical expressions involving whole-number exponents.
CCSS.Math.Content.6.EE.A.2 Write, read, and evaluate expressions in which letters stand for numbers.
CCSS.Math.Content.6.EE.A.2.A Write expressions that record operations with numbers and with letters standing for numbers. *For example, express the calculation "Subtract y from 5" as 5 - y.*
CCSS.Math.Content.6.EE.A.2.B Identify parts of an expression using mathematical terms (sum, term, product, factor, quotient, coefficient); view one or more parts of an expression as a single entity. *For example, describe the expression 2(8 + 7) as a product of two factors; view (8 + 7) as both a single entity and a sum of two terms.*
CCSS.Math.Content.6.EE.A.2.C Evaluate expressions at specific values of their variables. Include expressions that arise from formulas used in real-world problems. Perform arithmetic operations, including those involving whole-number exponents, in the conventional order when there are no parentheses to specify a particular order (Order of Operations). *For example, use the formulas $V = s^3$ and $A = 6s^2$ to find the volume and surface area of a cube with sides of length s = 1/2.*
CCSS.Math.Content.6.EE.A.3 Apply the properties of operations to generate equivalent expressions. *For example, apply the distributive property to the expression 3(2 + x) to produce the equivalent expression 6 + 3x; apply the distributive property to the expression 24x + 18y to produce the equivalent expression 6(4x + 3y); apply properties of operations to y + y + y to produce the equivalent expression 3y.*
CCSS.Math.Content.6.EE.A.4 Identify when two expressions are equivalent (i.e., when the two expressions name the same number regardless of which value is substituted into them). *For example, the expressions y + y + y and 3y are equivalent because they name the same number regardless of which number y stands for.*

Reason about and solve one-variable equations and inequalities.

CCSS.Math.Content.6.EE.B.5 Understand solving an equation or inequality as a process of answering a question: which values from a specified set, if any, make the equation or inequality true? Use substitution to determine whether a given number in a specified set makes an equation or inequality true.

CCSS.Math.Content.6.EE.B.6 Use variables to represent numbers and write expressions when solving a real-world or mathematical problem; understand that a variable can represent an unknown number, or, depending on the purpose at hand, any number in a specified set.

CCSS.Math.Content.6.EE.B.7 Solve real-world and mathematical problems by writing and solving equations of the form $x + p = q$ and $px = q$ for cases in which p, q and x are all nonnegative rational numbers.

CCSS.Math.Content.6.EE.B.8 Write an inequality of the form $x > c$ or $x < c$ to represent a constraint or condition in a real-world or mathematical problem. Recognize that inequalities of the form $x > c$ or $x < c$ have an infinite amount of solutions. Represent solutions of such inequalities on number line diagrams.

Represent and analyze quantitative relationships between dependent and independent variables.

CCSS.Math.Content.6.EE.C.9 Use variables to represent two quantities in a real-world problem that change in relationship to one another; write an equation to express one quantity, thought of as the dependent variable, in terms of the other quantity, thought of as the independent variable. Analyze the relationship between the dependent and independent variables using graphs and tables, and relate these to the equation. For example, in a problem involving motion at constant speed, list and graph ordered pairs of distances and times, and write the equation $d = 65t$ to represent the relationship between distance and time.

Solve real-world and mathematical problems involving area, surface area, and volume.

CCSS.Math.Content.6.G.A.1 Find the area of right triangles, other triangles, special quadrilaterals, and polygons by composing into rectangles or decomposing into triangles and other shapes; apply these techniques in the context of solving real-world and mathematical problems.

CCSS.Math.Content.6.G.A.2 Find the volume of a right rectangular prism with fractional edge lengths by packing it with unit cubes of the appropriate unit fraction edge lengths, and show that the volume is the same as would be found by multiplying the edge lengths of the prism. Apply the formulas $V = l \times w \times h$ and $V = b \times h$ to find the volumes of right rectangular prisms with fractional edge lengths in the context of solving real-world and mathematical problems.

CCSS.Math.Content.6.G.A.3 Draw polygons in the coordinate plane given coordinates for the vertices; use coordinates to find the length of a side joining points with the same first coordinate or the same second coordinate. Apply these techniques in the context of solving real-world and mathematical problems.

CCSS.Math.Content.6.G.A.4 Represent three-dimensional figures using nets made up of rectangles and triangles, and use the nets to find the surface area of these figures. Apply these techniques in the context of solving real-world and mathematical problems.

Develop understanding of statistical variability.

CCSS.Math.Content.6.SP.A.1 Recognize a statistical question as one that anticipates variability in the data related to the question and accounts for it in the answers. *For example, "How old am I?" is not a statistical question, but "How old are the students in my school?" is a statistical question because one anticipates variability in students' ages.*

CCSS.Math.Content.6.SP.A.2 Understand that a set of data collected to answer a statistical question has a distribution which can be described by its center, spread, and overall shape.

CCSS.Math.Content.6.SP.A.3 Recognize that a measure of center for a numerical data set summarizes all of its values with a single number, while a measure of variation describes how its values vary with a single number.

Summarize and describe distributions.

CCSS.Math.Content.6.SP.B.4 Display numerical data in plots on a number line, including dot plots, histograms, and box plots.

CCSS.Math.Content.6.SP.B.5 Summarize numerical data sets in relation to their context, such as by:

CCSS.Math.Content.6.SP.B.5.A Reporting the number of observations.

CCSS.Math.Content.6.SP.B.5.B Describing the nature of the attribute under investigation, including how it was measured and its units of measurement.

CCSS.Math.Content.6.SP.B.5.C Giving quantitative measures of center (median and/or mean) and variability (interquartile range and/or mean absolute deviation), as well as describing any overall pattern and any striking deviations from the overall pattern with reference to the context in which the data were gathered.

CCSS.Math.Content.6.SP.B.5.D Relating the choice of measures of center and variability to the shape of the data distribution and the context in which the data were gathered.

Mathematical Practice Standards

CCSS.Math.Practice.MP1 Make sense of problems and persevere in solving them. Mathematically proficient students start by explaining to themselves the meaning of a problem and looking for entry points to its solution. They analyze givens, constraints, relationships, and goals. They make conjectures about the form and meaning of the solution and plan a solution pathway rather than simply jumping into a solution attempt. They consider analogous problems, and try special cases and simpler forms of the original problem in order to gain insight into its solution. They monitor and evaluate their progress and change course if necessary. Older students might, depending on the context of the problem, transform algebraic expressions or change the viewing window on their graphing calculator to get the information they need. Mathematically proficient students can explain correspondences between equations, verbal descriptions, tables, and graphs or draw diagrams of important features and relationships, graph data, and search for regularity or trends. Younger students might rely on using concrete objects or pictures to help conceptualize and solve a problem. Mathematically proficient students check their answers to problems using a different method, and they continually ask themselves, "Does this make sense?" They can understand the approaches of others to solving complex problems and identify correspondences between different approaches.

CCSS.Math.Practice.MP2 Reason abstractly and quantitatively.
Mathematically proficient students make sense of quantities and their relationships in problem situations. They bring two complementary abilities to bear on problems involving quantitative relationships: the ability to *decontextualize*—to abstract a given situation and represent it symbolically and manipulate the representing symbols as if they have a life of their own, without necessarily attending to their referents—and the ability to *contextualize*, to pause as needed during the manipulation process in order to probe into the referents for the symbols involved. Quantitative reasoning entails habits of creating a coherent representation of the problem at hand; considering the units involved; attending to the meaning of quantities, not just how to compute them; and knowing and flexibly using different properties of operations and objects.

CCSS.Math.Practice.MP3 Construct viable arguments and critique the reasoning of others. Mathematically proficient students understand and use stated assumptions, definitions, and previously established results in constructing arguments. They make conjectures and build a logical progression of statements to explore the truth of their conjectures. They analyze situations by breaking them into cases, and can recognize and use counterexamples. They justify their conclusions, communicate them to others, and respond to the arguments of others. They reason inductively about data, making plausible arguments that take into account the context from which the data arose. Mathematically proficient students are also able to compare the effectiveness of two plausible arguments, distinguish correct logic or reasoning from that which is flawed, and—if there is a flaw in an argument—explain what it is. Elementary students can construct arguments using concrete referents such as objects, drawings, diagrams, and actions. Such arguments can make sense and be correct, even though they are not generalized or made formal until later grades. Later, students learn to determine domains to which an argument applies. Students at all grades can listen or read the arguments of others, decide whether they make sense, and ask useful questions to clarify or improve the arguments.

CCSS.Math.Practice.MP4 Model with mathematics. Mathematically proficient students can apply the mathematics they know to solve problems arising in everyday life, society, and the workplace. In early grades, this might be as simple as writing an addition equation to describe a situation. In middle grades, a student might apply proportional reasoning to plan a school event or analyze a problem in the community. By high school, a student might use geometry to solve a design problem or use a function to describe how one quantity of interest depends on another. Mathematically proficient students who can apply what they know are comfortable making assumptions and approximations to simplify a complicated situation, realizing that these may need revision later. They are able to identify important quantities in a practical situation and map their relationships using such tools as diagrams, two-way tables, graphs, flowcharts, and formulas. They can analyze those relationships mathematically to draw conclusions. They routinely interpret their mathematical results in the context of the situation and reflect on whether the results make sense, possibly improving the model if it has not served its purpose.

CCSS.Math.Practice.MP5 Use appropriate tools strategically. Mathematically proficient students consider the available tools when solving a mathematical problem. These tools might include pencil and paper, concrete models, a ruler, a protractor, a calculator, a spreadsheet, a computer algebra system, a statistical package, or dynamic geometry software. Proficient students are sufficiently familiar with tools appropriate for their grade or course to make sound decisions about when each of these tools might be helpful, recognizing both the insight to be gained and their limitations. For example, mathematically proficient high school students analyze graphs of functions and solutions generated using a graphing calculator. They detect possible errors by strategically using estimation or other mathematical knowledge. When making mathematical models, they know that technology can enable them to visualize the results of varying assumptions, explore consequences, and compare predictions with data. Mathematically proficient students at various grade levels are able to identify relevant external mathematical resources, such as digital content located on a website, and use them to pose or solve problems. They are able to use technological tools to explore and deepen their understanding of concepts.

CCSS.Math.Practice.MP6 Attend to precision. Mathematically proficient students try to communicate precisely to others. They try to use clear definitions in discussion with others and in their own reasoning. They state the meaning of the symbols they choose, including using the equal sign consistently and appropriately. They are careful about specifying units of measure, and labeling axes to clarify the correspondence with quantities in a problem. They calculate accurately and efficiently, express numerical answers with a degree of precision appropriate for the problem context. In the elementary grades, students give carefully formulated explanations to each other. By the time they reach high school they have learned to examine claims and make explicit use of definitions.

CCSS.Math.Practice.MP7 Look for and make use of structure. Mathematically proficient students look closely to discern a pattern or structure. Young students, for example, might notice that three and seven more is the same amount as seven and three more, or they may sort a collection of shapes according to how many sides the shapes have. Later, students will see 7×8 equals $7 \times 5 + 7 \times 3$, in preparation for learning about the distributive property. In the expression $x^2 + 9x + 14$, older students can see the 14 as 2×7 and the 9 as $2 + 7$. They recognize the significance of an existing line in a geometric figure and can use the strategy of drawing an auxiliary line for solving problems. They also can step back for an overview and shift perspective. They can see complicated things, such as some algebraic expressions, as single objects or as being composed of several objects. For example, they can see $5 - 3(x - y)^2$ as 5 minus a positive number times a square and use that to realize that its value cannot be more than 5 for any real numbers x and y.

CCSS.Math.Practice.MP8 Look for and express regularity in repeated reasoning. Mathematically proficient students notice if calculations are repeated, and look both for general methods and for shortcuts. Upper elementary students might notice when dividing 25 by 11 that they are repeating the same calculations over and over again, and conclude they have a repeating decimal. By paying attention to the calculation of slope as they repeatedly check whether points are on the line through (1, 2) with slope 3, middle school students might abstract the equation $(y - 2) \div (x - 1) = 3$. Noticing the regularity in the way terms cancel when expanding $(x - 1)(x + 1)$, $(x - 1)(x^2 + x + 1)$, and $(x - 1)(x^3 + x^2 + x + 1)$ might lead them to the general formula for the sum of a geometric series. As they work to solve a problem, mathematically proficient students maintain oversight of the process, while attending to the details. They continually evaluate the reasonableness of their intermediate results.

Grade 6 Common Core Score Report

After students take the Smarter Balanced Assessment, their results are reported in two different ways. Students will receive a scaled score and an achievement level score. The scaled scores vary by grade level. The sixth-grade scaled scores are shown on the following table.

Mathematics

Grade	Level 4	Level 3	Level 2	Level 1
6	>2,609	2,552–2,609	2,473–2,551	<2,473

Based on their scaled score, students fall into one of four categories of performance called achievement levels:

- Exceeded Standards—Level 4
- Met Standards—Level 3
- Nearly Met Standards—Level 2
- Did not Meet Standards—Level 1

Each year, Smarter Balanced Score Reports are sent home. As a parent, it is important that you go through the scores with your child as soon as you receive them. The score reports are designed to help parents and teachers better understand a student's progress in grade-related standards. These score reports also measure a student's readiness for future skills as he or she prepares for college or a career.

Achievement levels are only one measure. They should not be interpreted as a predictor of a child's future. Achievement levels must be continuously validated and should be used only in the context of the multiple sources of information that educators have about students and schools.

Index